# JUSTICE IN LATIN AMERICAN THEOLOGY OF LIBERATION

·

## Ismael García

*537*

John Knox Press
ATLANTA

Acknowledgment is made for permission to quote from the following sources:

To Cambridge University Press for excerpts from Walt Whitman Rostow, *The Stages of Economic Growth,* 1962; copyrighted by and reprinted with the permission of Cambridge University Press.

To Clarendon Press for excerpts from David Miller, *Social Justice,* copyright 1976 by Clarendon and used with permission.

To William B. Eerdmans Publishing Company for excerpts from José Míguez Bonino, *Christians and Marxists: The Mutual Challenge to Revolution,* copyright 1976 and used by permission.

To Fortress Press for excerpts from José Míguez Bonino, *Doing Theology in a Revolutionary Situation,* copyright © 1975 by Fortress Press and reprinted with permission.

To Fawcett for excerpt from Rudolfo Stavenhagen, "Seven Fallacies About Latin America" in *Latin America, Reform or Revolution?* ed. James Petra and Maurice Zeitlin, copyright 1968 and used with permission.

To Harvard Educational Review for excerpts from Paulo Freire, *Cultural Action for Freedom,* copyright © 1970 by the President and Fellows of Harvard College. All rights reserved. Used with permission.

To Orbis Press for excerpts from Gustavo Gutiérrez, copyright 1973 and used with permission.

**Library of Congress Cataloging-in-Publication Data**

Garcia, Ismael, 1947–
    Justice in Latin American theology of liberation.

    Revision of thesis (Ph.D.)—University of Chicago, 1982.
    Bibliography: p.
    1. Christianity and justice—History of doctrines—20th century. 2. Liberation theology. 3. Theology, Doctrinal—Latin America—History—20th century. I. Title.
BR115.J8G37    1987          241'.62          87-2787
ISBN 0-8042-0501-9

# PREFACE

•

This book is a revision of my doctoral dissertation, and like every study it is the product of the community of students from which it emerged, although the author is solely responsible for what is said. Among those who have contributed to my academic formation, I would like to express my gratitude to the faculty members of the Ethics and Society Field of the Divinity School of the University of Chicago: Professors Alan Anderson, Alvin Pitcher, and Gibson Winters. I am equally grateful to those persons who read and criticized the study at its early stages: Professors James M. Gustafson, Alvin Pitcher, and David Tracy. Special thanks are due to Professor Gustafson who directed my dissertation. From him I learned the value of and need for critical thinking, for listening to one's critics, and something that has been very important in my teaching career, for respecting, trusting, and encouraging the thinking of others. I can only desire to be as good a teacher for others as he has been for me. Finally, I am grateful to the two generations of students of the Ethics and Society Field who provided a supportive and challenging environment in which to work.

I wish, further, to express my appreciation to the Divinity School of the University of Chicago, the Ford Foundation Fellowship Committee, and the Fund for Theological Education for the financial assistance provided me at various times. Particular thanks are also due to The Association of Theological Schools for the financial support they gave me through their Younger Scholars Grants. Their support enabled me to travel and complete my research while visiting a number of Central American theological seminaries. The quite comprehensive revision of this project was possible because of their support.

The faculty of McCormick Theological Seminary, through their example of discipline and scholarly work, provided much incentive to finish both the dissertation as well as this revision. I also deeply appreciate the work of Maggie Newman, who diligently and accurately typed many drafts and the final form of this work.

Finally, I wish to express my gratitude to Maria Lina Collazo. She has been a faithful and supportive companion in this venture. Her sense of discipline, her organizational skills, her editing of various drafts, her contributions to the basic ideas of the work, and her critical comments have nourished its growth and enabled its final appearance. For the love she has given I can only respond in kind.

# CONTENTS

•

# INTRODUCTION

•

Questions of justice are central to the pastoral and theological work of Latin American liberation theologians. They frequently use the term, and readers of their works are well aware that justice issues are central to their theological reflection. Although their work is theological in the classical sense of that word, with the help of economists, political scientists, anthropologists, sociologists, and others within the social sciences, the liberation theologians reconsider traditional theological themes in the light of their experience of the faith.

The economic, social, and political realities of Mexico, the Central American countries, and the nations of South America have been described and diagnosed in a wide variety of ways. Numerous solutions have been offered. Pervasive, however, is the sense of injustice in the face of the extreme economic exploitation and political repression found in so many of these nations. Thus one finds in the liberation theologians an underlying ethical concern. They are deeply involved in the struggles for justice now taking place within many of the Latin American nations.

Liberation theologians, however, do not give us an explicit definition of justice. Our political, ethical, and theological traditions use the term with significant variations in meaning; differences in languages, cultures, and social understandings also charge the concept of justice with diverse shades of meaning. Thus, it is important to explain one's meaning when using the word.

This study has a twofold purpose: (1) to clarify what "justice" means to four major liberation theologians, and (2) to describe the implications of their understanding of justice for their economic and political life. All of the elements needed to construct a clear and consistent theory of justice are implicit in the work of these men. I intend to make explicit their concept of justice by presenting the arguments they use. It is also my contention that I can find enough resources within the work of these theologians to make a constructive argument and to formulate some concrete proposals for the just ordering of the economic and political realms.

I will examine the works of Hugo Assmann, José Míguez Bonino, Gustavo Gutiérrez, and José Porfirio Miranda. Assmann was born in Brazil. With a doctorate in theology, he has taught at the Jesuit theological seminary in Sao Leopoldo and at the pontifical Catholic University of Porto Alegre, Brazil. He has served as coordinator of studies at the Sao Paulo Institute of Philosophy and Theology, as well as a faculty member at the University of Münster in West Germany. In the field of sociology he has studied the Christian presence in the guerrilla movement in Teoponte, Brazil. Having studied mass communications as well, he has taught journalism in Costa Rica. A key figure and organizer of many gatherings for theological reflection, Assman is sometimes considered the "public relations" person for liberation theology.

Míguez Bonino was born in Argentina and did his first theological studies there. He later studied and served as a visiting faculty member at Emory University and Union Theological Seminary in New York City. An ordained Methodist minister, he has served churches in Argentina and Bolivia. At present he serves as dean of post-graduate studies at the Evangelical Institute of Advanced Theological Studies in Buenos Aires, Argentina. Míguez Bonino has distinguished himself as a key figure in the ecumenical movement, serving as an observer for the Methodist Church at Vatican II and serving on various boards of the World Council of Churches. He is by far the best known and most influential non-Roman Catholic among the liberation theologians.

Gustavo Gutiérrez has been called the "father of Latin American liberation theology." His book *A Theology of Libera-*

*tion* remains the classic statement of this mode of theological reflection. A Peruvian Roman Catholic priest, Gutiérrez studied theology and philosophy in his homeland as well as at the University of Louvain at Lyon, France, and at the Gregorian University in Rome. He now teaches at the Catholic University in Lima, Peru, and is advisor to the National Union of Catholic Students.

José Porfirio Miranda was born in Mexico. He studied economics at the universities of Munich and Münster before receiving a degree in biblical studies from the Biblical Institute in Rome. He always brings a socioeconomic expertise to his exegesis, but his sociological insights are not purely theoretical. He has been very active with worker and student movements in Mexico. Of all the theologians discussed, Miranda is the most distant from the church and organized religion, yet he provides one of the most articulate expressions of the ethical content of Scripture within the liberation movement in Latin America.

These four were chosen as central to the movement, representative of both Roman Catholic and Protestant perspectives, and expert in both theology and social analysis. They also all make use of the sociological theory of dependence to interpret the sociopolitical and economic realities of Latin America. The theory of dependence—as developed by such figures as Aníbal Quijano, Fernando Cardoso, Theotonio Dos Santos, Enzo Falleto, and André Gunder Frank—sees the underdevelopment of the poor nations not as a stage in their development toward the position First World nations have achieved but as a necessary corollary of the economic development of the First World. First World prosperity is built on Third World poverty. Liberation theologians' use of this sociological option in itself reveals a concern with justice and makes this concern explicit.

Other authors in this theological movement—Juan Luis Segundo, Enrique Dussel, and Rubem Alves—have been excluded from this study either because their social ethical concerns center around an issue other than justice (Rubem Alves, for example, is primarily concerned with freedom), concerns about justice are of secondary importance to them, or they do not add a new dimension to our understanding of justice. Their works, however, do constitute important secondary sources.

I will begin the study by considering how these theologians' theological method influences both the form and content of their thinking about justice. In the first chapter I will examine how they deal historically with the relation of justice to human rights. This historical consciousness is one of the main characteristics of their mode of theological reflection.

In chapter two I will consider in detail three levels of meaning in the term "liberation." It will then become apparent that the concept of justice is refined in each of these distinct but mutually interrelated levels of meaning. Here we find all the elements of the liberation theologians' understanding of justice. The first level provides through sociostructural analysis their understanding of the scope and proper concerns of justice. It enables us to determine what justice is by pointing at the unjust. The second level will enable us to understand the anthropology and value system that is normative for liberation theologians. It will also provide us with their vision of the good society. The third level provides us with the theological convictions that inform their faith and ultimately grounds their understanding of justice.

In chapter three I shall compare dominant alternative concepts of justice that liberation theologians consider. Chapters four and five attempt to articulate in a constructive way some implications of their concept of justice for the ordering of the economic and political realms. Chapter four deals with issues of economic justice such as property ownership, economic democracy, the right to work, and various legitimate criteria for economic distribution. Chapter five addresses the issues of political justice, such as democracy, the question of power, the right to freedom, and the nature of the common good.

I hope that the reader will not only be able to grasp the concept of justice but will also more fully understand its far-reaching implications for the lives of millions of Latin Americans for whom *injustice* is an everyday reality.

PART I

•

# JUSTICE
# IN
# THE CONTEXT
# OF
# LIBERATION

•

# 1
# THE CENTRALITY OF JUSTICE IN LATIN AMERICAN THEOLOGY OF LIBERATION

•

Liberation theology is that form of reflection that attempts to discern the religious significance of the sociopolitical struggles in which the poor are engaged as they free themselves of their present state of political domination and economic exploitation. It is the practical theology that has accompanied the emergence, clarification, and consolidation of a new sociopolitical and historical project that has been slowly but steadily captivating the minds and hearts not only of Latin Americans but of the Christian community as a whole. The reality of mass poverty and political powerlessness to which the people of Latin America have been subjected and their struggles to overcome this burden are seen as religiously significant events, events that raise once more the question of what it means to be a Christian and what it means to be a church in today's world.

The language of liberation did not emerge from within the church. It is a thoroughly sociopolitical language, the language of the fronts of national liberation, revolutionary political movements, and the new Latin American Marxism. As Christians committed themselves to these struggles, as they identified with the hopes and aspirations of the poor, they began to discover the language of liberation and reappropriate their faith and tradition (Scripture, creeds, theology) in a new way, cleansing them of servitude to the structures of oppression and domination and revising the liberating and empowering elements of the gospel that have often been suppressed and distorted.

Liberation theology differentiates itself from other modes of theology not only by its religious and theological affirmations but by its sociopolitical option and commitment. Its uniqueness is based primarily on its political option for the poor, making them and their struggle a focus from which to engage in meaningful theological reflection.

In a continent such as South America, the challenge does not come to us primarily from the nonbeliever but from the nonperson, that is to say, from the person who is not recognized as such by the existing social order: the poor, the exploited, those who are systematically deprived of being persons, and who scarcely know that they are persons. The nonperson questions before anything else, not our religious world, but our economic, social, political, and cultural world. Thus, the call is for the revolutionary transformation of the very basis of a dehumanizing society.

This contextualized form of theological reflection attempts to respond to what it considers religiously significant human problems while actively participating in the processes by which people attempt to solve them. It strives to avoid turning concrete human problems into abstractions. Hence, as it reflects on the issue of massive human suffering, it looks at the concrete manifestations of poverty itself within the specific sociohistorical coordinates of a given country. It also attempts to participate in those social movements that attempt to overcome poverty. It assumes the ambiguities and limitations of the political options of the context. Although there are similarities in the experience of domination and exploitation that most of humanity experiences, this is not maintained at the expense of the differences that make the experience of domination and exploitation in one country different from that of another. It refuses to remain marginal to the political movements that can provide a viable solution.

Liberation theologians are suspicious of the theological work done by colleagues who live and think their faith in radically different sociohistorical circumstances. Their suspicion denies neither the value and contribution of such work nor their own personal indebtedness to the theological and pastoral work done within rich nations. Such works are intrinsic to their religious tradition. Their suspicion, however, does make them aware of undue claims of universality and absolute validity explicitly or implicitly found in most theological works. For them, an authentic appropriation of the tradition is much more than the mere preservation and repetition of what was experienced and formulated in the past or in another context. It demands a reformulation, a purification, as it were, of the distortions that result not only from the sociohistorical limitations of the author in question—the limitation of vision and understanding natural to every finite creature—but also from the personal and collective sin of which everyone is part. Furthermore, for liberation theologians, it is extremely important to remain conscious of the exclusion or absence of the poor (the majority within the Christian community) from the selection and formulation of a significant number of works that have become classics of our Christian faith and life.

Neither the past nor the present can determine the nature and scope of theological concerns or the range of the solutions to the problems Latin American Christians confront. The uncritical acceptance of theological constructions has made most theological reflection in Latin America both irrelevant and insensitive to the reality of misery and powerlessness experienced by most of the people of this region. As liberation theologians began to break with "the parasite me" mentality of neocolonial Christianity and with the "cultural imperialism" under which most Latin American Christian intellectuals live, as they claimed their right to "misread their teachers" and find their "own interpretation of their theological task,"[1] they have made the global church conscious of the priority the reality of mass suffering has for theological reflection and church life. Even more significantly, they have made their own churches aware of the fundamental meaning theological thinking has for politico-historical liberation. Gustavo Gutiérrez expresses this with an insight and passion that merits quoting at length:

An oppressed and believing people have a right to think. And doing theology is participating in this right to think—a right to think one's faith in the Lord, a right to think one's liberating experiences. This right also includes the right to reappropriate the faith—the faith which is constantly ripped away from the oppressed people—in order to turn it into an intellectual justification of the situation of domination. Thinking the faith also includes the right to reappropriate the Bible, which is usually read from the point of view of the dominators. It is, finally, the right to reappropriate one's own theological reflection.

In this light, doing theology from the perspective of an oppressed and believing people is one part of their right to liberation. Because, we must not forget, reflection is also an historical power; it is a way of holding power in history. And this is a right, I believe, in the perspective in which we are working, which our people demand more and more. This is the reason, it seems to me, why the wish spreads, the wish to interpret, to think, to become conscious of one's faith and one's situation. In this perspective, doing theology is an expression of the rights of the poor. (In this connection, more and more in Latin America we prefer to speak of the rights of the poor, not of human rights. That is to say, we do not wish to speak of rights in the liberal and bourgeois sense, but in terms more biblical, and more conflictual, too, it is true.)[2]

. . . The theological endeavor, from a point of departure in (and through the actual agency of) the exploited, pertains to their right to liberation. We dare not forget that all reflection is a way of exercising power in history. It is only one way, of course, but it is a real way. It makes a real contribution to the transformation of history—to the destruction of the system of oppression and the construction of a just and humane society. Reflection on the faith as lived in this struggle is a necessary condition for the proclamation of the living God from a pulpit in the midst of the poor.[3]

It must be clear how questions of social justice and human rights are at the center of this form of theological reflection. It is not unreasonable to define this theology as being a form of critical reflection, in the light of faith, on the historical praxis through which men and women seek the creation of a new and more just state of affairs. Liberation theology emerged within a context that revolves around an injustice/justice axis. It cannot be conceived apart from issues such as the distribution of wealth and power and the concrete realization of the most elementary human rights. By necessity it must raise the critical political problem of how to do justice effectively in the world today.

The practical quest for a just society has become a new basis of ecumenism among liberation theologians, an ecumenism that includes not only persons of different religious traditions and beliefs but also nonbelievers as well. The urgency of the struggle for justice has prompted these theologians to accept the need to relativize some of their religious and philosophical differences. They have found a common practical task that has priority and is undertaken in spite of theological differences. Still this has not meant a surrender of values and insights of their particular traditions. These are also recognized as essential to true ecumenism.

Although the issue of social justice is central to the reflection and practice of liberation theologians, they never present a clear statement of what they mean by this frequently used term. My intention in this chapter is to draw upon those explicit and implicit sources found in their works that will enable us to formulate what they mean by justice, what criteria give their notions of justice content, and how they justify their views.

I shall begin this study by considering some key aspects of the content, main assumptions, and theological method of liberation theologians. This will enable the reader to arrive at some formal dimensions of how liberation theologians think about justice. Afterward I shall consider the meaning of the term *liberation* as it unfolds in three levels of meaning. This will give a sense of the way they deal systematically with ethical issues, the substantive or material content they give to the term *justice,* and the ethical and theological arguments they present to justify their claims. This will point to what is unique in the liberation perspective on justice. I shall conclude by comparing the concept of justice presented by liberation theologians with the natural law concept of justice central to the Roman Catholic tradition, the natural rights concept of justice central to liberal capitalism, and the positive law concept of justice that predominates in practical legal thinking in the West today.

## Theological Method

Liberation theology is not an elaboration of a new theological theme, the theme of liberation, but a new way of doing theology. It is theology done "where the pulse of history is beating, . . . within the vicinity of strategy and the tactical sphere of human activity."[4] Its constant point of reference is the historical praxis of men and women, particularly Christians, as they seek to transform the world and create a just society that enhances the freedom and well-being of the poor.

The method is depicted as a never-ending dialectic between theory and practice, i.e., a hermeneutical circle between the concrete sociopolitical and historical praxis of the community of faith and its interpretation of Scripture, the theological tradition, and in particular its interpretation of God's historical presence. Through this dialectic the theologian allows himself/herself to be questioned by the challenges people confront in their quest to create a more humane and just world. These challenges become occasions for the theologian and the community of faith at large to begin a process of self-criticism, reinterpretation, and reappropriation of essential elements of our religious faith. They are also occasions for discovering new and hidden facets of revelation, giving new direction to the pastoral mission of the church.

The method makes theologians aware that they are never just observers of history but always historical actors. Their reflection is always reflection about and from within a sociopolitical commitment. Theologians must recognize the mediated and contextualized nature of their reflection, of their reading of Scripture and the tradition. They must always recognize that their religious reflection cannot avoid embodying a particular ideology and historical option.

The method also characterizes theology, like the historical task itself, as a never-ending process. It seeks to liberate theological reflection from undue dogmatism. No theological formulation can claim any more permanence, certainty, or universality than any other form of human reflection. Theological reflection must not only be focused on historical praxis but also must come to terms with its own historicity and, thus, its contingent and provisional character. If this makes theological reflection somewhat relative, it does not necessarily condemn Christian thought to radical relativism.

While this theological method enables theologians to be thoroughly anthropological, sociopolitical, and historical in their religious reflection, it also seeks to enable them to be *seriously theological*. While theologians must allow themselves to be challenged by new events and aspirations and informed by the wisdom of the world through which these challenges are explained and solved, they cannot afford merely to accommodate themselves to the world and accept its wisdom uncritically. If, for example, the historical praxis of liberation becomes an occasion to reexamine the faith and pastoral mission of the religious community, then the religious community itself must appeal to its own religious and theological criteria to judge this historical praxis and to contribute to giving it direction. The religious tradition is itself a source for correcting distortions and pointing to shortcomings in the struggle for liberation. This critical dimension might very well have been awakened by one's openness to the challenge presented by the liberating struggle. Its content, however, was not created *ex nihilo*. Critical criteria have always been an intrinsic part of the life of faith. Liberation theologians see the symbol of the kingdom of God as one that provides normative criteria, direction, and content to the historical quest for social justice. It provides principles that are more illuminating than prescriptive, pointing the way rather than specifying how to arrive at it, but which definitely call us to a quality of life with justice.

Liberation theologians, thus, do not deny that our theological tradition and Scripture do provide criteria, principles, and guidance for our collective actions. They do reject, however, the idea that we can understand the meaning of these principles and apply them to our situation in a direct and immediate way. Ethical criteria—including biblically informed ethical criteria—are not grasped in all their depth a-temporally, but only in relation to the concrete conditions of existence of men and women historically situated. Further, we arrive at a more comprehensive understanding of such concepts as justice, love, peace, and reconciliation as we actively participate in the process of bringing them about.

Since we can never have immediate and certain knowledge of where God's kingdom dwells and what God's purpose is, we can never justify our concrete sociopolitical options as being the only ones that agree with the faith. Such knowledge is always mediated and very much subject to human fallibility. The best we can claim is that our views and options seem not to contradict God's purpose as revealed in Scripture and understood by tradition. We are obliged to remain attentive to the views of others as we proceed to assert our basic convictions on these matters. The community of faith is obligated to be a community of sociopolitical discourse. Other Christians have chosen other options.

> What are we to make of that? . . . these options entail mediating factors: theological interpretation, scientific analysis, and ideological synthesis. All such mediating factors are human and fallible, and so I cannot absolutize my option eschatologically. But neither can I take refuge in mere relativity. Either one or the other option is in error on this continent, at this point in history; or else there is some third option, not an abstract one but a concrete, viable one in real life.[5]

Only in a polemical context, then, can we recognize the existence of other options. We must invite our fellow human beings to join us in analyzing our theological and sociopolitical mediations, so that we may be able to join together in professing God's reign in word and deed. To do anything else would be to denigrate either one's fellow human beings or one's witness of God's rule.

In the perspective of this methodology, truth and knowledge are found and verified in their practical realizations, through their capacity to transform the world. Knowledge results from one's active engagement of and relationships with reality. A liberating form of reflection is not an end in itself, but must encourage an ever-more-resolute commitment to the struggle for liberation. The priority given to praxis, however, must not make us oblivious to the dialectical nature of the method, its relationship to fundamental thought, and the dignity of the activity of thinking itself. Action without reflection is as distorted and incomprehensible as reflection in abstraction from a concrete commitment. Critical reflection is very much a praxis.

For this mode of thinking the political is an "always," not just an "also." Theologies that seek to be politically marginal or neutral—claiming to be concerned exclusively with the religious and spiritual development of persons—support the status quo. It is better and more truthful to be conscious and intentional regarding one's political option than to engage in unconscious politics.

On the contrary, faith gives more depth and meaning to political existence. The political dimension intrinsic to our faith in no way deprecates the purity of faith. Rather it makes the political more dynamic and future oriented. Our faith contains a radical critical dimension that does not allow us to be completely satisfied with any particular sociopolitical configuration, even the most progressive and revolutionary. Yet, it does this without making irrelevant the significance of the historical task of struggling for the realization of one particular socioeconomic and political order, as opposed to another. One's political options are not ultimate, but they do have significance in terms of the ultimate: God's realm of peace and justice as the end of dominations of persons over persons.

It is clear that "there is no *divine* politics or economics" and thus "that we must resolutely use the best *human* politics and economics at our disposal."[6] No one has the right to argue that one's analysis of the present state of affairs and one's prescribed solutions to solve its problems are directly derived from Scripture or the theological tradition. Neither of these provides by itself enough resources to construct a sociopolitical program or to decide which among the available programs is the best. We should not "force biblical authors to deal with issues that were of no concern to them . . ." nor "ask them questions that they did not ask themselves."[7] Political options and social analysis are primarily a matter of scientific rationality. Their selection, while it must agree or be consistent with our theological convictions and commitments, must be justified rationally. A theology engaged in the struggle for social justice, thus, needs to use the tools and procedures provided by the social sciences.

Between normative theological convictions and commitments and the concrete historical options we confront in solving issues having to do with our sociopolitical life, there must exist the mediation of the social sciences. They enable us to move beyond the level of sentiment and sheer moralism. "No sentimentalism can replace the sober assessment of the situation . . ."; one "must avoid moral indignation clouding the nature of the issue."[8] Only a structural and dialectical analysis of reality can provide theologians with an interpretation of the dynamics and conflictual nature of social reality, enabling them to effectively participate in its transformation toward the realization of justice and human rights.

The social sciences also enable theologians to do their own theological task and pastoral work more thoroughly. They can, for example, make the community of faith aware of how its beliefs and practices help either to support or change the social order, and they offer a sense of how the community's beliefs and practices either encourage or suppress the struggle for freedom and well-being for and with the poor. Thus, the social sciences can help the community of faith realize its ethos of creative involvement in the liberation of humanity.

## Assumptions

The main assumption which informs the methodology of the liberation theologian is a wholistic or unitary understanding of human existence and history. A major weakness of many theologians has been the establishment of a gap between human history proper and salvation history, i.e., between the sacred and the profane. Another major weakness of contemporary thought has been the establishment of fixed and mutually exclusive boundaries between the different realms of human existence, i.e., the economic, the social, the political, the cultural, the religious, etc. Liberation theologians seek to formulate a theology that overcomes these divisions. On the basis of this assumption they can meaningfully raise the question of the relationship that exists between the creation of a more just world and the kingdom of peace and justice; about "the relationship between salvation and the process of the liberation of man throughout history? Or more precisely, what is the meaning of the struggle against an unjust society and the creation of a new man in the light of the Word?"[9]

Liberation theologians claim that when a gap is established between historical praxis and its ultimate religious meaning another more finite source of meaning will take the place of the religious and claim for itself an ultimacy that more properly belongs to the religious. In such circumstances, the community of faith is in danger of losing the sense of urgency about the struggle for justice and can also lose sight of its responsibility for advancing the work of creation to the end given to it by God, the realization of God's kingdom of peace and justice.

It is important to differentiate the various realms of human existence. This will make us more aware that each one of them has an integrity of its own and that the problems they embody must be dealt with in accordance with their specific characteristics. The struggle for liberation has many dimensions. It is impossible to assume that because we have dealt with one of its aspects, the problems of others are solved. For example, the struggle for socioeconomic and political liberation does not automatically bring forth the psychological liberation of individuals. This latter form of liberation must be dealt with in its own terms.

Although distinctions are necessary, they must not make us oblivious to the fundamental dialectical interrelationship and unity of all dimensions of human existence. It is important to see

how the realms of human existence are dialectically related to
each other.

Furthermore, no dimension of human existence remains
marginal to the religious. It is impossible to attempt to establish
boundaries and limits to the forms and places where God can
be revealed to us. God is and remains the ultimate meaning of
human existence in all realms and activities of human existence.
The political, although secondary, also has this broad universal
character. It is the realm where men and women struggle to
find and fulfill meaning; no human activity remains outside the
political. While the political always remains penultimate, it also
is intrinsic to ultimate meaning.

All forms of dualistic thinking are conservative and support
an unjust state of affairs. They imply a disregard for both the
task of creating history and the possibility of forwarding the
freedom and well-being of the poor and marginal. Dualistic
modes of thought misplace the axis of ethics on an ideal plane
and free, by this act, all realms of history to the manipulation
of established power. In synthesis, dualisms are the political
ideology of order and the status quo.

## Content

The methodology used by theologians of liberation is not
neutral or merely formal. Like any other theological method, it
implies a particular political option and a particular historical
project. It is a reflection within the context in which the poor
struggle to create a more just society. It is a partisan reflection,
done from the perspective and for the benefit of the poor and
those who unite with them and through them for the benefit of
all humanity. The poor and their struggle to create a new social
order are the necessary contents of this theological method.
This content becomes the hermeneutical principle from which
to understand Scripture, the tradition, and the pastoral mission
of the church:

> If theology is to be a reflection from within, and upon, praxis,
> it will be important to bear in mind that what is being reflected
> upon is the praxis of liberation of the oppressed of this world.

> To divorce theological method from this perspective would be
> to lose the nub of the question and fall back into the academic.
> It is not enough to say that praxis is the first act. One must
> take into consideration the historical subject of this praxis—
> those who until now have been the absent ones of history.[10]

The needs of the poor and the creation of a new society that
will enable them to overcome their poverty and domination
serve as the criteria by which these theologians choose among
the social sciences. It must be a partisan social science seeking
ways to transform the status quo at its roots so that those who
were oppressed can become artisans of a new social order.
Thus, it must be a social science that does not allow itself to be
co-opted by the present status quo. Liberation theologians have
made an option for Marxism as their social analytical tool (they
reject orthodox Marxism and are critical of all Marxist social
science that is done from the perspective of the nondependent
nations). They choose the theory of dependence, which is a
reformulation of sociological Marxism, done from the perspective of poor nations, and as original a form of Marxism as the
new socialist society they are in quest of. Marxism for them
provides the only radical critique of capitalist accumulation and
an adequate analytical framework capable of projecting the
need of a new social order as a requirement for justice. It also
has a "prophetic" dimension which is not completely in contradiction with their religious tradition.

The liberation of the poor will ultimately verify the validity
and authenticity of both the social sciences and theology. What
Gustavo Gutiérrez says about theology also applies to the social
sciences: what is ultimately at stake is not doing theology but
liberating the poor.[11] Both theology and the social sciences are
most authentic when they become the expression of the action
and reflection of the poor in their quest for liberation.

## Thinking about Justice

On the basis of the observations we have made so far, we
can determine some essential elements in the way liberation
theologians think about justice. They reject any consideration

of justice that is abstract and ahistorical. The idealistic procedure of first attempting to clarify what justice is and then seeing
how it can be applied to present circumstances is rejected.
Instead, they approach the question of justice in a political and
contextual fashion. The problems, possible solutions, and priority questions are determined in terms of the concrete social
relationships that prevail within the community and in light of
the experiences people confront within the particular sociohistorical coordinates in which they are struggling to bring about
a just state of affairs. On this basis one can build and test the
adequacy of a large theoretical frame of reference. This approach, they argue, is more consistent with the biblical approach. What justice consists in and what it entails are best
known by reflection on the thinking and practice of those who
struggle for its realization.

Our understanding of justice and human rights is always
partial and incomplete. We can never claim to have exhausted
what justice entails. The realization of justice, as well as our
understanding of it, is a historical task, a slow and cumulative
process with "many steps, with apparent failures that after-
wards result in tremendous relevance for their long term efficacy."[12] We have an obligation to assume a posture and be
zealous about its defense, while remaining open to revision and
reformulation. We can never adopt a position valid for all times
and circumstances.

The quest for justice and human rights is radically historical. At different times groups with very different histories have
struggled for different freedoms and rights. Each struggle
represents a contribution, leaving a permanent imprint on our
present understanding of what a just state of affairs is. The old
and the new achieve new levels of synthesis.

Among the theologians we are studying, Gustavo Gutiérrez
and José Míguez Bonino have explicitly dealt with the issue of
justice and human rights from a historical perspective. They
trace what Hegel has called the "history of freedom" in the
Western world. From it, they stress those historical events they
believe have left a permanent imprint on the way the commu-

nity of faith has formed its own particular understanding of justice and human rights. They argue that we cannot speak of a Christian understanding of human rights and justice as something which would have developed autonomously or in isolation from the historical happenings that surround it. A dialectical interaction exists in which historical experiences stimulate Christians to explore, question, and reappropriate the sources of their faith. This, in turn, inspires them to commit themselves more vigorously to the struggle for human rights and justice.

The first historical event liberation theologians identify as having made a permanent impact on the Christian understanding of justice and human rights is the struggle with the Roman government by early Christian families for religious freedom. They fought both for freedom of conscience and for freedom to practice the religion of their choice. This struggle represented an assertion of religious autonomy and thus a struggle both to limit the areas of state intervention and to deny the competence of the state in religious matters. Even though these struggles were carried out as a matter of self-interest by Christians and even though Christians violated these principles when theirs became the political theology of the status quo, their claims to freedom of conscience and the right to practice the religion of one's choice have remained a permanent contribution to the Christian concepts of freedom and human rights.

The second set of historical events that had a permanent impact on the Christian understanding of human rights and justice were the North American and French revolutions. The vanguard in these struggles was the emerging capitalist bourgeoisie who conceived the struggle for human rights and justice in nonreligious and even antireligious terms. The rights for which this new social class struggled were much broader than the freedom of conscience and religious practice. They sought to secure the right of the individual to freedom in all dimensions of life, not only in the religious but also in the economic, social, and political realms. They demanded freedom for the individual to exercise his or her self-determination and the right to determine how she or he ought to live. They rejected all forms of external or heteronomous interventions, whether by secular or religious authority. The individual became the main center of authority. The church's authority was to be limited to religious life. Even there, it was also to be subjected to the scrutiny of each individual conscience. The state was also to be limited in its area of intervention and competence; its sphere was to be held to a minimum. Its main function was to protect and secure the broadest space and freedom possible for each individual to pursue his or her interest as she or he saw fit. It could only intervene in a person's actions and decisions when those violated the rights of others. The main concern of the American and French constitutions was and is the protection of the rights of the individual.

Individualism, universality, and formal equality are the distinct marks defining the bourgeois concept of human rights and justice. The individual is an "absolute beginning, an autonomous center of decisions"[13] in all dimensions of life. Human rights "are defined in this stage in the perspective of the individualism that characterizes modern thought."[14]

Individual interests became the basis of economic activity as well. All individuals must be allowed to use their talents and resources in whatever way will render greater benefit for them. The marketplace must also be free from all political and religious intervention. It must be allowed to regulate prices and gains by the law of supply and demand so that the natural balance between the individual and the general interest takes place. These views lead to a purely procedural concept of justice: whatever distribution results from voluntary dealings between people in the free market is just as long as there has been no undue manipulation of the system, no use of force or coercion in the contracts engaged in, and no violation of the prevailing system of law.

Individuals must also have freedom assured so they can decide about what kind of society to live in. In this way they will have a greater measure of assurance that it will be a society where freedom will not only be respected but also maximized. All genuine authority, thus, has the individual's consent at its basis, and all persons are seen as bearers of these inalienable rights and, as such, as equals.

The attitude of the community of faith to this broadening of human rights was at best ambiguous. Ever since the fourth century when Christians became the religion of "the establishment," they have always expressed an ambiguous and largely negative attitude regarding the struggle for social justice and the broadening of any understanding of human rights. Politically speaking, the religious establishment has been and still is by and large a conservative institution. The Roman Catholic Church at first rejected the bourgeois historical project because it represented a threat to the church's position of power and authority. The church was concerned that people would drift away from religious truth, endangering not only the stability and unity which Catholicism gave to the political community but also their personal salvation.

The Roman Catholic Church was so dependent on the aristocracy and its government that it became blind to the intrinsic affinity between the early Christian claims for freedom in the act of faith and the modern claim for freedom of conscience in all aspects of life. Only a sector of the Catholic Church participated in the struggle to forward modern freedom. Protestants had fewer problems recognizing the continuity of the struggles of the past and modern freedoms, partly because they saw these freedoms as an integral part of their own demands for freedom over against the Roman Church.

Liberal bourgeois capitalism proved itself an irreversible historical project. The Roman Church, while practically abiding by the new system, continued to oppose it in theory for a long time. However, both the church and the bourgeoisie gradually began to reconcile their differences. They saw the benefits to be derived from the new economic order as well as the threat of the emerging proletariat. Here was an independent social class with its own historical project, a view of the good society, and a demand of radical transformation of bourgeois society. Not until Vatican II did the Roman Church come to fully recognize, proclaim, and support liberal free-

doms and rights. The growing acceptance of modern freedoms by the community of faith has enabled it to unveil a
religious basis within its own sources and tradition from which
to argue for the unconditional worth and respect due to each
individual as an individual.

> It is this Christian element that gives to Christians a strong basis
> to stand for human rights in the critical situations which are
> faced today . . . securing a firm basis for the universality of
> human dignity and right. It is not necessary to rehearse here
> the vast amount of theological work that has been done in this
> respect. It has rested basically on the doctrine of creation and/
> or the doctrine of redemption. The human being as God's crea-
> tion and image, his/her dignity as God's steward and repre-
> sentative, the unity of the human race constitute a strong basis
> for asserting the rights of all. On the other hand, the Incarna-
> tion, the universal love of God attested by and operative in
> Christ's death and resurrection, the dignity of a humanity
> which in Christ has been exalted at the right hand of God,
> indicate an ultimate and unwavering commitment of God him-
> self to the human being which underlies the value—the "infi-
> nite value" as classical liberal theology used to say—of each
> human being.[15]

The third and final historical period that has left a permanent imprint on the Christian understanding of justice and
human rights is the ongoing struggle for socioeconomic rights,
the rights of well-being, carried out by those who were excluded from or who remain marginal within the benefits of
liberal capitalism. These struggles were first carried out by industrial workers. More recently, since the industrial nations
have become capable of co-opting the proletariat of their nations, the vanguard in the creation of a new society and world
economic order are the poor and marginal nations of the Third
World. For the theologians of liberation, these are the new
proletariat who have the historical mission of creating a new
social order.

Social rights, in contrast to traditional civil and political
rights, require that the state intervene and aid in acquiring
those goods and services necessary to achieve a secure and
dignified life. Meeting the basic needs of life now appear as a

necessary condition for the meaningful and concrete realization of civil and political rights.

Christians who have committed themselves to these struggles for social justice have found an opportunity to reappropriate the prophetic tradition of their faith and rediscover how the struggle for justice is intrinsic to concern for the poor and for Christian discipleship and identity.

From this historical survey of the main events that have shaped the Christian conscience on justice and human rights, Míguez Bonino can discern an "ethos" concerning God's relationship to humanity in history, pointing in the direction of "a search for a 'more human life,' for the fulfillment, within the conditions of history, of the best material and spiritual possibilities available for the human person and society."[16]

Christianity, as a monotheistic religion, proclaims a belief in the existence of one God, Parent of all humanity. This belief serves as the basis for a view of the unity of the human family and the intrinsic worth and respect owed to each individual as a creative being in the image of the Creator. The view that each person is a son or daughter of God and a brother or sister of Jesus has radical consequences for a life of Christian praxis. It demands a radical commitment to humankind as a way of expressing love to God and loyalty to divine purpose.

> The consequence cannot be avoided: there is only one mankind ... all are one body, in which all members have equal dignity and value: social, ethnic, cultural, even sexual distinctions ... cannot justify any discrimination. But this universality overflows the limits of the community. Every human being bears the image of God; it is therefore absurd and sacrilegious "to bless the Lord and Father ... and to curse men, who are made in the likeness of God."[17]

God is also viewed as having the preservation of human life as one of the key purposes of creation and salvation. In Assmann's view, God is found within the historical process through which persons struggle to appropriate nature for the preservation of a life worthy of the name human. As Míguez Bonino declares:

> Human life is still the key to creation. . . . God's "covenant" with man has "life" and particularly "human life" as its fundamental content. He is unconditionally and absolutely the God of life. And consequently, he entrusts man with a mission: the perpetuation, enriching and protection of life. This is God's most precious treasure, so much so that not even his just and necessary wrath against man's sin is cause enough to annul the alliance. When the decisive time comes the God-made-man will protect the human race with his own life. He will take upon himself the just punishment and the senseless violence of the fallen world so that men may live.[18]

Finally, liberation theologians claim that the needs of the poor provide the material content for the formal definition of justice: to render to each his or her due or to treat equals equally and unequals unequally. The satisfaction of the needs of the poor becomes the criterion by which to measure the justice of a given state of affairs. Insofar as justice has to do with guaranteeing and forwarding the rights of freedom and well-being, that is, political and socioeconomic rights, the rights are to be interpreted from the perspective of the needs of the poor.

> It is one of the deepest insights of the Biblical picture of God that his universality finds concrete expression in his "partiality" in favour of the poor. . . . At this point the biblical concept of justice parts company with the classical tradition. It is not the "blind" rendering "to each his own"—which presupposes a stable and basically unchangeable order—but the liberation of those who have been deprived of the conditions for an authentic human life. Such a vision does not mean a rejection of universality. . . . There are always historical tests for universality. In biblical terms, this test is the condition of the poor. Here we have the basis for a deeper understanding of the struggle for human rights. . . .
> . . . As the slogan of "human rights" becomes one of the rallying points today in the world, it is of paramount importance for us to bear this historico-theological test in mind. For the vast majority of the population of the world today the basic "human right" is "the right to a human life." The deeper meaning of the violation of formal human rights is the struggle to vindicate these large masses who claim their right to the means of life. The defence of formal human rights is meaningful as a

pointer to that deeper level. In that sense, the drive towards universality implicit in our Christian faith, which found partial expression in the quest of the American and French revolutions, the aspirations expressed in the UN Declaration finds its historical focus today for us in the struggle of the poor, the economically and socially oppressed, for their liberation. At this point the biblical teaching and the historical junction coalesce to give the Christian churches a mission. This is the reason why "Christians should be concerned with human rights."[19]

Justice and right cannot be emptied of the content bestowed on them by the Bible. Defending human rights means above all defending the rights of the poor. It is a prophetic theme, and one deeply rooted in the tradition of the church. And it must be kept in mind in order to avoid falling into the liberal focus with regard to human rights. The liberal approach presupposes, for example, a social equality that simply does not exist in Latin American societies.

It is this approach, and not the defense of the poor, that inevitably leads to the particularisms and ideologization that some fear today within the Latin American church. Our understanding of the true meaning, and biblical requirement, of the defense of human rights will originate with the poor of Latin American society. Here is where we shall begin to grasp that this task is an expression of the gospel proclamation, and not some subtle form of power-grabbing, or presenting a program as a political alternative in Latin America. The church does not recive its prophetic inspiration from adherence to a liberal program, but from its roots in a world of poverty.[20]

For liberation theologians supplying the needs of the poor becomes the uncompromising end and ultimate purpose of the struggle for human rights and social justice. It is the basis on which the community of faith has to define its historical praxis. In Miranda's view, "in order that the moral imperative of justice, in which God consists, might arise in history, only one thing is needed: the otherness of the neighbour who seeks justice." He continues:

In reality, all that is needed for the imperative to arise is a person who needs our solidarity and our help, . . .
Only the summons of the poor person, the widow, the orphan, the alien, the crippled constitutes true otherness. Only

> this summons, accepted and heeded, makes us transcend the
> sameness and original solitude of the self; only in this summons
> do we find the transcendence in which God consists. Only this
> summons provides a reason for rebellion against the masters
> and the gods in charge of this world, those committed to what
> has been and what is.[21]

The needs of the poor give the never-ending historical struggle for justice a direction that saves it from the danger of relativism. Every act for their well-being and freedom contains within itself the announcement and realization of history's ultimate meaning. In Gutiérrez's words, "The abolition of the exploitation of man by man is something possible, . . . efforts to bring it about are not in vain, God calls us to it and assures us of its complete fulfillment, . . . the definite reality is being built in what is transitory."[22] Miranda agrees: "Within history, there is an *eschaton,* an *ultimum,* toward which all the partial realizations of justice are directed."[23] The needs of the poor give a concrete and measurable content that frees the struggle for human rights from becoming mere abstract formulations. They also give justice and the struggle for human rights a more universal scope since they address the needs of most of humanity.

Only insofar as the value of human equality becomes visible within the socioeconomic and political realms will it become possible to speak meaningfully of the dignity and respect due to each individual as a person. The respect for human dignity must be measured by the treatment society gives to its poor and marginal. Thus, as long as there are poor, the goals of social unity and equality remain goals to be achieved. The poor make us aware of the incompleteness and imperfection of the status quo.

In terms of the problem of justice, the unitary conception of human existence that liberation theologians uphold implies that in principle the rights of freedom and the rights of well-being enjoy an equal standing. They are interrelated in such a way that neither one is a mere means to the other. Each contributes to the realization and preservation of the other. Historically, these rights must be ordered in light of concrete sociohistorical circumstances. Neither of them can be disregarded, nor can it be assumed that the satisfaction of one will automatically satisfy the other. In the liberation perspective both must be realized.

# 2
# LIBERATION AND JUSTICE
•

The term *liberation* is used by Latin American theologians in a broad and comprehensive way. It expresses the longing to be free from all that represents a significant limitation to the realization of one's potentialities as well as the desire to be free to realize one's potential to the fullest. The term also has significance in relation to the struggle for social justice. In Gustavo Gutiérrez's words, the process of liberation "highlights the profound aspirations which play a part in the struggle for a more just society."[1]

The term *liberation* describes a single but complex process which has three distinct and dialectically related levels of meaning: economic and sociopolitical liberation, historico-utopian liberation, and religious liberation. To grasp, in a more systematic way, how liberation theologians deal with questions of social ethics in general, and with the issue of justice in particular, one must see how justice relates to each of these levels. Each level unveils a dimension of justice unique to it, as well as the main ethical and theological beliefs and arguments these theologians use to justify their views. These levels enable us to trace the way their argument moves: from a description and evaluation of the social circumstances in which they minister, to the formulation of key ethical and political principles and their notion of human nature, and finally, to the formulation of theological convictions and a description of the ideal life of the community of faith.

FIRST LEVEL:
# Economic and Sociopolitical Liberation

At the first level the language of liberation is negative. It is a language of denunciation, change, and discontinuity emphasizing the need to transform society at its roots so that a more equitable distribution of wealth and power can take place. This level of scientific rationality points to what is unjust regarding the present state of affairs. It does not tell us what is just except indirectly by telling us what is unjust. Given the present state of Latin American nations this seems to be the most adequate starting point.

> The concerns of the so-called Third World countries revolve around the social injustice-justice axis, or, in concrete terms, the oppression-liberation axis. . . . In the underdeveloped countries one starts with a rejection of the existing situation, considered as fundamentally unjust and dehumanizing. Although this is a negative vision, it is nevertheless the only one which allows us to go to the root of the problems and to create without compromises a new social order, based on justice and brotherhood. This rejection does not produce an escapist attitude, but rather a will to revolution.[2]

In presenting the statistical figures depicting the disparity between levels of growth among rich and poor nations, the trade deficit, the overconcentration of land in the hands of the few, foreign control of key sectors of the national economy, inequitable income distribution, unemployment, literacy rate, and health services and conditions, liberation theologians have at least two purposes in mind. First, they seek to describe the condition in which the majority of the people of this hemisphere live, a fact which is significant to any serious theological reflection. Second, they appeal to the reader's sense of justice. This is an attempt to awaken that feeling of injustice all conscientious human beings experience when they are confronted with the extreme and massive social misery and hardship that are intrinsic to the reality of underdevelopment.

The feeling of injustice can be described as that capacity

we have to recognize and react negatively when we see people being deprived of what belongs to them, subjected to extreme socioeconomic and political inequality, and systematically denied their conceptions of the good life. We can identify with them and understand their misery, in a partial way, by this empathy we call the sense of injustice. It enables us to understand the injustice that exists and to take more resolute steps toward making a commitment to participate in the process of overcoming it. For the community of faith this is a well-known experience.

Informed and efficient action cannot, however, rely solely on the feeling of injustice. We need a structural understanding of how society works. Political action must be guided by the rationality of the various social sciences which enables us to formulate descriptions and prescriptions for social change. The feeling of injustice and scientific rationality work synergistically. The feeling of injustice prevents scientific rationality from becoming merely technical and calculative; it keeps us aware that its subject matter is human beings, who have both worth and dignity. Scientific rationality, on the other hand, enables us to make our feelings and value commitments historically viable by giving us a sense of causal relations, hidden possibilities, and the limitations of a given state of affairs.

Liberation theology has distinguished itself by its interdisciplinary work with the social sciences. More particularly, it has distinguished itself, in its quest to understand its sociohistorical coordinates, by adopting the sociological theory of dependence.

> Commitment to the process of liberation in Latin America means starting from a particular analysis of our situation as oppressed peoples; that opting for a particular social analysis is not a neutral step. It involves the necessary choice of an ethical and political stance; there is no such thing as an uninvolved social science, and to pretend that there is is itself to adopt a reactionary ideological position. . . . There is probably no more obvious example of a committed science anywhere today than sociology in Latin America, which has taken the decisive step

of making "dependence" the central theme of its investigations into the real situation in Latin America. This situation of dependence is the basic starting-point for the process of liberation. On the theological level an analysis of dependence has produced the language of the theology of liberation.[3]

In order to grasp the relevant issues central to a liberation understanding of justice, we must understand the main tenets of dependence theory. To do this we must see this theory in its proper historical setting.

Dependence theory is a response to alternative theories of development, in particular to the structural functionalist approach developed in Europe and North America, the various revisionist versions of structural functionalism developed by Latin American social scientists, and the autonomous nationalist development view which has come to be known pejoratively as "developmentalism." The theory of dependence has sought to present not so much a new theory of development as a new theoretical approach to and perspective on understanding the unique way development has manifested itself in Latin America. My examination is limited to the works of Theotonio Dos Santos, André Gunder Frank, Aníbal Quijano, Fernando H. Cardoso, and Enzo Faletto, the social scientists who have greatly influenced the works of the theologians with whom we are dealing. Although there are differences between these social scientists, by and large, they share a general framework of reference and assumptions.

I am dealing with a group of countries quite different in culture, tradition, and socioeconomic and political development. In my attempt to describe these nations as dependent I seek to present only the general framework that delimits the possibility of their growth and development. The way particular nations are in fact limited by the structure of dependence will vary significantly. Dependence and underdevelopment thus do manifest themselves differently in different countries, although the main characteristics of these phenomena can be described in a general way.

From Developmentalism to the Theory of Dependence

Modern theories of development are concerned with self-sustained and rapid economic growth. This is what ultimately will enable a country to maximize production, broaden the distribution of wealth and services, democratize the political realm, distribute power more equitably, integrate different sectors of society, and affirm and develop the nation's heritage. In spite of these general agreements there are still significant differences as to the ways development can take place.

## *Structural Functionalism*

Within Europe and North America, the structural functionalist approach to development predominates. Development is seen as entailing a process of continuous transformation within a harmonious movement of social differentiation and reintegration of functions. The history and the experiences of development of England and North America are presented as a normative example of this process. It is assumed that all nations can learn from these experiences and that they can and should follow a similar process if they are ever to modernize and achieve a higher level of growth and well-being.

Methodologically, the theory proceeds either by creating a system of ideal-type constructions which attempt to describe the essential characteristics (or pinpoint the essential variables) that define developed and underdeveloped societies or by attempting to establish, in equally abstract terms, the historical stages which depict the passage rich nations underwent in their journey from underdevelopment to development.

In the first case, a program of development is established by incorporating those variables characteristic of developed nations which are still absent in underdeveloped nations by removing those variables that are characteristic of underdevelopment and thus an obstacle to the process of self-sustained growth. The actualization or elimination of key variables becomes the core and purpose of the development project. The variables can be structural ones, such as the free market system, a particular form of organizing production, or the institutionalizing of social mobility; or they can be more subjective, such as a given value system, religious belief and practice, or attitudes toward work and leisure. Since the perspective upon which these evaluations are made is that of the now developed nations, Latin American societies are usually described in negative terms, that is, as societies lacking some key variable essential to an industrial society: capital, technology, organizational skills, stable political institutions, or a value system that creates inner dispositions appropriate to a modern industrial state. By transforming one or a number of these variables, the process of development can be stimulated. This perspective never questions the social structure as a whole. It assumes that the structure will gradually and more or less harmoniously develop once the missing variables are introduced or once the obstacles are removed. Radical social change is seen as both economically and politically inefficient and costly.

The historical model attempts to arrive at a definition of the "historical stages" a nation must go through in its movement from a backward to a modern industrialized society. Here too, an attempt is made to determine the relevant factors that can become catalysts in forwarding development. It is assumed not only that one can formulate such stages but also that poor nations can in fact follow the same historical process. Walt Rostow presents the classical statement of this perspective:

> It is possible to identify all societies, in their economic dimensions, as lying within one of five categories: the traditional society, the preconditions for take-off, the take-off, the drive to maturity, and the age of high mass-consumption.
> A traditional society is one whose structure is developed within limited production functions, based on pre-Newtonian science and technology, and on pre-Newtonian attitudes towards the physical world.
> The second stage of growth embraces societies in the process of transition; that is, the period when the preconditions for take-off are developed; for it takes time to transform a traditional society in the ways necessary for it to exploit the fruits

of modern science, to fend off diminishing returns, and thus to enjoy the blessings and choices opened up by the march of compound interest.

. . . the stage of preconditions arises not endogenously but from some external intrusion by more advanced societies.

The take-off is the interval when the old blocks and resistances to steady growth are finally overcome. The forces making for economic progress, which yielded limited bursts and enclaves of modern activity, expand and come to dominate the society. Growth becomes its normal condition. Compound interest becomes built as it were, into its habits and institutional structure.[4]

The structural functionalist believes that the passage from a traditional to a modern society is not difficult. Development is relatively easy. The transition is further facilitated by the presence of the industrialized nations and the already industrialized sectors within the poor nations themselves. Both of these are willing sources of capital, technology, and organizational skills to help the impoverished nation or sector develop.

Structural functionalists tend to view Latin American societies as "dual societies," nations with an archaic feudal structure existing side by side with a modern capitalist sector. The feudal sector, seen as a remnant of the Spanish and Portuguese conquest and colonization, is identified as the main cause of underdevelopment. It is what stifles the process of social evolution. Its backwardness is due mainly to its isolation from the modern industrialized world. In contrast to the supposed feudal sectors, the more developed regions within the poor nation are seen as examples of what can happen when an impoverished area has contact with the modern world. It is this contact that will initiate the process of gradual but sustained economic growth.

Many Latin American social scientists have appropriated the methodology and the working assumptions of the structural functionalists. This is understandable when one considers that they have been educated and trained in the First World. It is also important to point out that since the nineteenth century there have been Latin American politicians, economists, and humanists who have viewed the United States as a model to imitate and follow. Many of the constitutions of these nations were drafted along the lines of the North American and French constitutions. These, together with England, were identified at the time as progressive societies very much concerned with the well-being of humanity as a whole.

At present, however, we do find significant changes in the ways Latin American social scientists view the structural functionalist method. They now argue that the experience of development of North Atlantic nations does not provide the Latin American nations with a proper framework or model provoking thought about their own development. It is erroneous to define Latin American nations in terms of the experience of the developed nations. The framework of the developed nations ignores the problems that are unique to the Latin American nations who have also become suspicious of the work done by social scientists who are contented with the structure of the society they study, never thinking to question the status quo.

Latin American social scientists find it very difficult to accept the status quo of the society they study. The reality of underdevelopment and the misery it entails make it difficult even for conservative social scientists who have any professional integrity to formulate a sociology of the establishment. It is difficult for them not to give the issue of social change priority in their work.

For the most part Latin American social scientists have changed their point of reference and have focused on their own societies and their unique histories. This approach has enabled them to arrive at a more adequate understanding of the causes of underdevelopment, political instability, continuous economic crisis, and chronic unemployment. Still many of them have found it difficult to abandon some of the assumptions that are part of the functionalist perspective. It is still difficult for many to conceive of social change in terms other than gradual, evolutionary change. The "stages of growth" mentality has taken hold of many of them. Gino Germani provides one of the clearest examples of this.

The political evolution of Latin American countries can be described in a succinct way as a series of six successive stages, and consequently the present state of each country can be defined in terms of the stage already reached within the process of transition. It is not necessary to point out the dangers involved in this procedure. Nonetheless, it is the only process that enables a view of the process as a whole, and as long as its obvious limitations are kept in mind, it is a methodological resource of considerable usefulness.

The six stages in which we divide the process are the following: (1) Wars of liberation and the formal proclamation of independence; (2) civil wars, "caudillismo," anarchy; (3) unifying autocracies; (4) representative democracies with limited participation or oligarchy; (5) representative democracies with broad participation; (6) representative democracies with total participation; and as a possible alternative to the above mentioned democracies, popular national revolutions.[5]

## Developmentalism

Raul Prebisch, the ideological mentor of the United Nations Economic Commission for Latin America (ECLA) took a more definite stand against the historical stages and some of the main tenets of the structural functionalist approach. Although categorized as a "developmentalist," he still remained committed to some of their assumptions. He made a significant contribution to the understanding of Latin American underdevelopment by linking it to the international economic system. For him the world economy is divided into two main areas: an "industrial center" specializing in the production of industrial goods and a "periphery" specializing in the production of agricultural goods and other raw or primary goods. The trade patterns established between these "equal" partners have generated benefits for the center and benefits to a small sector of the peripheral nations but have not enabled the latter to initiate a process of self-sustained growth. There has been a constant deterioration of the terms of trade for the exporter of primary goods. These are constantly falling in price while the prices of the goods produced in the metropolitan industrial center are constantly rising. This has contributed to making it impossible for the peripheral nation to accumulate capital for its own industrial development. If these economic forces were left to themselves, then they would most likely lead to the constant deterioration and backwardness of the poor nation.

To stop and reverse this process, Prebisch argues, it is necessary to engage in a conscious and deliberate program of industrialization headed by the state. This can be achieved through a process of import substitution, so that poor nations may have access to those necessary capital goods to develop their own industry. The state is to direct this effort but always with the help and support of the private sector. The state will enact policies of import control and tariff protection; it will give preferential treatment to national industries over foreign ones. Without state intervention, poor nations will not be able to compete as equals with national economies whose wealth and power transcend not just the influence of their own states but also the economies of the poor nations. For Prebisch it is clear that development will not result from the dynamics of the free market but only from the mobilization of social forces guided by the state.

Prebisch is aware that steps must be taken to guard against discouraging positive foreign contributions in order to overcome "the technical inferiority of the domestic enterprise because it weakens the initiative of the executives and thus does not encourage them to improve their techniques."[6] Foreign aid and technological assistance are indispensable for the periphery to develop, but in providing technology and capital, the rich nations must listen to the recommendations of the recipient nations. It is important that the rich nations open their markets to the products produced by poor nations, that is, reduce significantly their protectionist policies and give preferential treatment to the goods produced by poor nations. Given their present economic strength, this would not bring upon them any significant hardship.

Prebisch's concern with the deterioration of trade patterns does represent a significant contribution toward a reinterpretation of the causes of Latin America's underdevelopment. However, he does not consider a number of relevant questions. He does not ask about the particular interests and needs of the developed nations. The interests of their ruling classes are not taken into account even though they are essential to an understanding of the central policies of these nations. Nor does he take into account the particular interest of the dependent nations' ruling classes, which does much to explain why they promote the policies they do. For Prebisch, underdevelopment has an external cause, the deterioration of trade relationships between rich and poor nations. To overcome this obstacle, it is important to change the conditions of trade, which for him is a goal that can be achieved without any basic structural transformation within the poor nation itself. His recommendation for the integration of various Latin American nations into a regional market and the policies of import substitution are predicated on the assumption that this region's underdevelopment can be overcome through a process of reforming the national and international capitalist structure. He never raises the question of whether or not there can be internal structural causes to the reality of underdevelopment that, if not changed, can make his recommendations a contributing factor in enhancing the underdevelopment of poor nations, rather than a contribution to forwarding their integral development.

Prebisch also seems to assume that the dependent nations' national bourgeoisies have the interest, intention, and power to enact policies for national development. He seems to believe that this class can break the power of the traditional oligarchies and overcome the external impositions of the industrial centers. He still conceives development in terms of finding ways to stimulate the passage from the present state of underdevelopment to a state more akin to the presently developed nations.

A more adequate description of the Latin American reality of underdevelopment is presented by Helio Jaguaribe.[7] Beyond the deterioration of trade patterns, which Prebisch emphasizes, Jaguaribe sees the underdevelopment of poor nations as the result of several factors: their economic stagnation; their marginality from the decision-making centers of the metropolitan or First World nations; the marginality of the rural areas from the urban centers within these nations and of most of the population from the mainstreams of society; their military, economic, and political dependence on the metropolitan center; and finally, the increased decapitalization and penetration by multinational corporations of the most advanced economic sectors of the poor nations' economies.

Jaguaribe argues that Latin American nations, depending on their present stage of development and their present structural conditions, have to choose among three alternatives for their future development. One would be to remain as they are and allow their increasing dependence and subordination to the metropolitan centers to continue. This is the alternative open to the weakest and poorest nations. For them the future promises little more than recurrent periods of crisis and instability. Second, they may engage in a revolutionary struggle that at best will change their dependence from capitalist to socialist. For them the future promises continued instability and dependence until a world socialist order is established. Finally, a few viable nations, the stronger ones that have more natural resources, can obtain autonomous development. For Jaguaribe this is the most promising and reasonable alternative.

If in the next ten years the viable Latin American nations—among them Brazil, Argentina, and Mexico—enact some significant changes such as a more equitable distribution of wealth and power, it is likely that in the next thirty years these nations could enter a process of autonomous and continued development. Other Latin American nations do not have the resources to achieve autonomous development, although through a process of integration with one of the viable states they could achieve a higher level of development.

Jaguaribe, like Prebisch, appeals to those in power to bring about the necessary changes that could forward the poor nations' development. He appeals, however, not to the national bourgeoisie but rather to an enlightened military elite which has middle class values and is technically and professionally well trained. It is this sector of the middle class that should have control of the state and lead the process of development. At present, he claims, no other social class can bring society together and channel its resources toward the objective of development. Only the military has the recognized authority and legitimacy as well as the expertise to fulfill this task.

He also assumes that development will result from the natural evolution of the present system, once the proper reforms are enacted. The national and international capitalist order is seen as flexible enough to allow for slow but continuous change. Tampering with the system is not only costly, but it is likely to bring more hardship than well-being. Thus, we do better by changing the ideology and value system that informs the practices of those in power than changing the system itself. Jaguaribe more than other developmentalists is aware of the national causes of dependence and not just the international ones. He agrees with them that reforming the present system is possible and is enough. There is no need for radical social change.

In reality, the expectations and goals of the policies of development supported by the metropolitan centers and the national bourgeoisies have been frustrated. They believed that the process of import substitution would reverse the trend of underdevelopment and enable the poor nations to industrialize. This process of rapid industrialization would itself alleviate the problem of marginality by enabling a larger sector of society to become integrated into the economic and political mainstream. Developmentalists also assumed that poor nations would be able to have a stronger international market and compete in the free market on more favorable terms. Politically, they expected poor nations to be able to exercise greater sovereignty over their local affairs and have a more active voice in those international processes that significantly affected them. A strong nation state and a democratic constitution were seen as natural outcomes of a stable economy and a continued process of economic growth. Finally, developmentalists expected that the technological gap between the rich and the poor would be overcome. Yet, development did not take place.

### Theory of Dependence

In contrast to structural functionalism and developmentalism, dependence theory begins with a more radical questioning
of the whole capitalist project. It raises the question of whether
or not there is an alternative and viable way for poor nations
and social classes to free themselves from the underdevelopment into which they are now forced. When the issue is politi-
cized, it is no longer a matter of accelerating the evolutionary
process of capitalist development but of radically transforming
the capitalist structure itself. The gradual and harmonious process of change and growth is abandoned for a political process
of social revolution. The only way to break away from the ties
of dependence and underdevelopment is to organize and empower the poor so that they may initiate a new historical project: the creation of a socialist and egalitarian society seeking to
satisfy its socioeconomic needs and its innermost political and
human longings.

Dependence theorists recognize that their theoretical approach is still an ongoing effort. At times, they work with broad
and general hypotheses whose verification goes beyond the
socioeconomic facts that serve as their basis. Their hypotheses
are not always tested propositions, although they are more and
more encouraged by the historical and sociological evidence
they are finding. Their aim is to provide a comprehensive
framework on which to formulate their hypotheses and unveil
underlying problems that many times are lost in case studies of
particular nations. For case studies to make sense they should
be done within the framework of a more comprehensive theory.

Dependence theory is the Latin American contribution
toward an understanding of the reality of the underdevelopment which these nations experience. It is a theory understood
from the perspective of the poor nations and with the purpose of enabling them and the social classes within them to liberate themselves from their present state of affairs. It is a
Latin American contribution to the Western understanding

of the phenomenon of imperialism as it affects poor nations.

According to this theory, in order to understand the phenomenon of underdevelopment we must place it in the context of the emergence, growth, and consolidation of the capitalist world economic system. The underdevelopment of poor nations is nothing but a particular experience of development within this historical process. The struggle to grasp this historical process is more important and relevant to a theory of development than the formulation of ideal types and historical stages. Development cannot be meaningfully conceived as the transition from an original stage to a particular goal, both of which are defined abstractly and ahistorically. Theotonio Dos Santos paraphrases it, describing the passage from a society that is not effectively known to one that will never exist. As soon as one assumes a historical perspective, one can overcome some of the anachronisms intrinsic to the functionalist model. Latin American societies will no longer be viewed as tribal or feudal societies living today at a stage of growth similar to that of seventeenth-century England. History cannot be conceived as unilinear, nor can it be assumed that poor nations can reenact the same processes that the now developed countries went through to achieve their present development. Or as Fernando Cardoso and Enzo Falleto put it,

> Methodologically, it is not licit to assume . . . that in the "developing" countries there is a repetition of the history of the developed countries. In fact, the historical conditions are different. . . . It is not enough to consider all differences as deviations from a general pattern of development, since all factors, forms of conduct and the economic and social processes, that at first glance appear as deviant or imperfect forms of realization of the classic pattern of development, must be seen as nuclei of the analysis destined to make intelligible the socioeconomic system.[8]

A historical perspective also makes us aware that when the European nations were industrializing, they were able to accumulate capital both by exploiting their colonial territories and by the exploitation of their own working class, including the exploitation of women and children. The enactment of laws for the expropriation of land together with antivagrancy laws assured industrialists a broad class of "free laborers" forced to work for low wages and under poor working conditions. At this time the internal markets of the now developed countries developed according to their internal needs. They were not subjected to the external pressures of a stronger nation. The ruling classes of these nations had the capacity to rule according to their own interest and well-being. The development of the nation was an intrinsic part of their own interest. Unexploited markets allowed opportunity for growth and for a more diversified exportation of raw materials, manufactured goods, and agricultural goods. Even when a country specialized in one area of production, it was able to complement the production of another country. Finally, when new techniques and other circumstances did not allow a country to give its people work, those who were excluded could emigrate and begin anew.

Latin American nations have tried to achieve their development under radically different circumstances. From the time of the Spanish colonization, these nations have been subjected to the direct or indirect domination of external markets. Their economic, social, and political life was organized to satisfy the needs of the imperialist nations. They began as agricultural exporters because this was what the dominant nations needed. Given today's labor unions and the legislation protecting their rights, the Latin American nations cannot subject their work force to the same kind of exploitation under which the work forces of seventeenth-century European nations suffered. They have never had colonies to exploit. Neither are there many markets for Latin American nations to use as profitable outlets for their surplus products. Even international trade today is less complementary since the industrial center is able to produce the same or similar products as those of the periphery. The integration of new techniques of production and other improvements in the economy that increase the problem of unemployment cannot be solved by the emigration of workers. More and more unskilled labor has no place to go. On the contrary, it is skilled and specialized labor that often leaves poor nations. Finally, the national ruling classes have neither achieved nor exercised autonomous decision-making power. They have always accommodated and identified their interests with those of the ruling classes of the rich nations. They have not been able to carry out an autonomous historical project similar to that of the bourgeoisie of the rich nations. It is unprofitable for them to identify their self-interest with the development and interest of their nation as a whole.

These comparisons demonstrate the inadequacy of the assumption that all pre-industrial nations are confronted with similar circumstances and ought to be able to follow a similar path of development. Besides, poor nations have not been absent from the historical process through which the now developed nations achieved their development. Neither poor nor rich nations have a history independent of one another. Development and underdevelopment have not been the result of the growth of autonomous nations but rather the product of the dialectic interrelationship between center and periphery within the limits of the capitalist world economic structure. They are two necessary sides of the same process.

The ideologists of the policies of autonomous national development, as we mentioned, saw the external causes that sustain the reality of underdevelopment. They saw that underdevelopment is in part the result of the role these nations play in the process of the international accumulation of capital. However, they did not see as clearly how this same international structure shaped the internal structure of the poor nations. The failure of their policies and programs should awaken the suspicion that poor nations are not only dependent on their external dealings with the developed nations, but that their internal structure itself is dependent as well. The international structure of subordination and domination has created within the poor nation an inner structure in its own image. All attempts to develop within this national and international framework necessarily result in a dependent form of development.

The condition of dependence is not a static one. It changes in correlation to the changes that world capitalism itself undergoes. Most dependence theorists agree with Dos Santos' division of this historical process into three main periods:

> (1) Colonial dependence, trade export in nature, in which commercial and financial capital in alliance with the colonialist state dominated the economic relations of the Europeans and the colonies, by means of a trade monopoly complemented by a colonial monopoly of land, mines, and manpower (serf or slave) in the colonized countries. (2) Financial-industrial dependence which consolidated itself at the end of the nineteenth century, characterized by the domination of big capital in the hegemonic centers, and its expansion abroad through investment in the production of raw materials and agricultural products for consumption in the hegemonic centers. A productive structure grew up in the dependent countries devoted to the export of these products . . . what ECLA has called "foreign-oriented development." . . . (3) In the postwar period a new type of dependence has been consolidated, based on multinational corporations which began to invest in industries geared to the internal market of underdeveloped countries. This form of dependence is basically technological-industrial dependence.[9]

Dependence is defined as a situation in which the economy of a given country is conditioned by the development and expansion of the economy of another country to which it is subjected. What is unique to the Latin American experience is that these nations were born as dependent nations. Thus their internal structure has been formed as that of dependent capitalist nations.

> Dependence, therefore, is a constitutive element of Latin American societies. In a different way, other societies like the Hindu society or pre-revolutionary China at one level, or Japan at another, became engaged in relations of dependence as already constituted societies and were capable of preserving their character as such throughout this process. The same cannot be said, for example, of the Aztec and Incan societies which were totally disintegrated as particular sociohistorical configurations, although their population and a number of isolated elements, even some structural nuclei of them, became an integral part of those societies that developed afterward in their territories.[10]

To understand the phenomenon of dependence and to define policies to overcome it, it is necessary to grasp the dialectical relationship that exists between the dominant metropolitan nations and their subordinate partners and the relationship that is established between dominant and subordinate social classes. In short, it is necessary to grasp both the external and internal dynamics that are intrinsic to this relationship.

## Underdevelopment:
### A Particular Form of Capitalist Development

Underdevelopment is not an original state or a condition all nations have experienced at one time or another. Rich nations were once *un*developed but they have not been *under*developed. Underdevelopment is a particular form of capitalist development, a form of dependent development that occurs within the historical process of the expansion and integration of all national economies into a world market of commodities, capital, and labor. It is the necessary but negative side of the same historical process through which the now developed nations arrived at their present condition of economic and political supremacy.

An integrated world economy is a desirable goal—a constructive step toward the establishment of a more efficient and equitable system of production, distribution, and consumption of available resources on a world scale. Very few nations are capable of autonomous, self-sustained development. Thus, most nations stand to gain from the fair integration of national economies. It would enable nations to contribute to each other's growth.

The experience of capitalist integration into a world economic order has been dominated by the narrowness of nationalist and private interests. It has resulted in power and wealth being concentrated in the hands of the few and misery and powerlessness in the hands of the many. Competition has resulted in domination, not in cooperation.

The domination that has taken place is not only external.

The ruling classes within poor nations have found it economically and politically advantageous to pursue policies which perpetuate their countries' dependence. Without the cooperation of this class or another social group, it would be impossible for the metropolitan center to exercise its dominion. This is the only way one nation can dominate another without resorting to military invasion. Domination usually is enhanced by the internal policies that a local ruling group enacts. The ruling class acts the way it does, not because it does not know better but because its actions assure it a high level of material gain and social advantage.

At present, Latin America's dependence on the United States for industrial and capital goods, sophisticated civilian and military technology, organizational skills, financial assistance, and other forms of aid has enabled the United States to infiltrate and dominate the most dynamic sectors of the poor nations' economies. This has resulted in a significant transfer of control over both economic and political decision-making power from the poor nation to the industrial nation.

Development requires more than the diffusion of capital from the rich to the poor nations. The amount of capital extracted from the periphery to the industrial center reveals that poor nations have the capacity to produce capital, but poor nations must be understood in a different context of development, a socialist context of development. Dos Santos declares:

> The only option or the only "valid alternative" . . . to the present economic policy, is a socialist policy, based on social mobilization, price control, control of profits of big industry, in the nationalization of the main sectors of the economy, in a radical land reform directed against land ownership that creates collective forms of exploitation of Brazilian agriculture.[11]

It is no longer possible for Latin American countries to achieve an independent capitalist form of development. This historical alternative ended with the failure of the policies of import substitution and the capitulation of the indigenous national bourgeoisie. Only by moving away from the capitalist context of development will poor nations have the possibility of achieving some level of integral development. However, it is not likely that total isolation from the hegemonic or dominant center will enable peripheral nations to enter a process of self-sustained growth. A policy of radical isolation not only fails to eliminate the condition of dependence but might very well radicalize the poor nations' internal crisis. Dependence can be overcome by a radical transformation of the social structure within the poor nation and an eventual transformation of the international structure as well.

As we have mentioned before, underdevelopment has been attributed to the existence of backward rural areas. In Latin America, this sector emerged and consolidated itself as a significant economic unit during the time of mercantile capitalism. It provided the agricultural goods and raw materials Spain and Portugal needed. It also supported the extraction of gold, silver, and other precious metals that took place during the colonization of this region. When England became the world hegemonic center, the agricultural sector grew even more since it was complementary to the manufacturing industry of the industrial center. An efficient organization for the production and trade of agricultural products and raw materials was established at this time by the Latin American oligarchy.

At present, the agricultural sector does represent a limit to the integral development of Latin American nations. The exchange between agricultural and industrial nations, as we have seen, is disadvantageous for the former. Further, agricultural production is no longer complementary but rather competitive with the North American agricultural sector, which is one of the most productive in the world. At the same time, the agricultural sector has sustained the industrialization of Latin American nations. It has provided the national bourgeoisie with the necessary financial resources as well as with a local and international market. This has made the survival of the agricultural oligarchy indispensable for the industrial bourgeoisie. No matter how antagonistic the interests between these classes are, they both recognize that it is to their mutual advantage to reach some compromise and to accommodate each other. They both agree that drastic social change would harm their interests.

Dependence theorists argue that the traditional agricultural sectors have in fact never been isolated from the mainstream of the historical process by which capitalism has expanded and consolidated itself. Further, they argue that the present state of poverty and backwardness this sector suffers is due precisely to the economic role it has played in this historical process. Poverty and backwardness do not cause underdevelopment but are themselves the products of underdevelopment. Once established, they support and forward underdevelopment even more.

> The progress of the modern, urban, and industrial areas of Latin America has taken place at the expense of backward, archaic, and traditional zones. In other words, the channeling of capital, raw materials, abundant foods, and manual labor coming from the backward zones permits the rapid development of these poles or focal points of growth, and condemns the supplying zones to an increasing stagnation and underdevelopment. The trade relations between the urban and the backward areas are unfavorable to the latter in the same way that the trade relations between underdeveloped and developed countries on a world scale are unfavorable to the underdeveloped countries.[12]

### Economic, Political, and Cultural Manifestations of International Dependence

The unequal and combined character of capitalist integration is what ultimately accounts for the position of economic and political subordination of Latin American nations in relation to the industrialized nations. While the international and national metropolis-satellite structure persists, these nations will not be able to free themselves from their underdevelopment and the misery and powerlessness it entails. From this perspective dependence theorists seek to understand the structural problems that plague Latin American nations: economic stagnation, marginality, and the continuous denationalization of wealth and power.

Underdevelopment manifests itself most clearly through the reality of economic stagnation. When one compares the development of Latin American nations with their European and North American counterparts, one gets the impression that at one point in history development came to a halt. In the mid-eighteenth century the development of both the now developed and now underdeveloped nations was more or less the same. The rate of illiteracy, infant mortality, and overall standard of living were very similar. A century later, however, the gap between them began to widen. Today it seems insurmountable.

Dependence theorists attribute this gap to the subordination Latin American nations were subjected to in the early stages of the expansion and consolidation of world capitalism and the exploitation and domination that resulted from it. Their development did not really stop but rather took place in the dependent development mode with all the distortions this entailed. The wars for national independence, and, more recently, policies to achieve industrial development have not rid Latin American nations of North American and European domination. In spite of the significant changes that occurred in the international relationships between metropolis and satellite, the economic growth of the satellite has remained a reflection of that of the metropolis. The possibility for a more self-sustained process of growth and development has been systematically denied. Compared to the nations in whose economic orbit they function, Latin American nations are significantly less developed, have less productive capacity, much lower consumption, and a more passive role in the decision-making process that affects them in significant ways.

Transnational corporations have been able to co-opt and dominate the most dynamic sectors of the economy. These economic conglomerates have a virtual monopoly over capital goods, technology, organizational skills, and other goods and services needed by local industry to function. Poor nations depend on them for the very possibility of a functional industry. Since 1950, foreign penetration has forced significant sectors of national industries to become subsidiaries and affiliates of these conglomerates. Thus, the transnational corporation has become the integrating center of all the major economic activities at both ends of the spectrum.

This economic superiority of foreign capital has enabled it to determine policy which itself sustains the process of decapitalization and overexploitation of profits. Payments made by the poor nation for industrial and capital goods, technology, and other economic and commercial services, as well as payments of the national debt to cover the balance of payment deficit, interest on loans, royalties and freights, are all factors contributing to the process of decapitalization.

The outflow of capital goes hand in hand with a loss of decision-making power at both the national and international levels. Whether the decisions are made by nationals or by foreign personnel, they represent policies that defend and consolidate the interests of the transnational corporations, at times even at the expense of the integral development of the poor nation.

This form of domination, like all forms of domination, needs to be justified and given a rationale. The dominant ideology, when looked at from the perspective of the poor, is a distortion of those cultural symbols and human longings through which a people attempt to express the meaning of their public being. The dependent society internalizes values and imitates a lifestyle which belongs to a radically different sociopolitical context. Thus, those in power speak of freedom, equality, justice, and the common good while the poor only have the illusion of experiencing these through the privilege and power of their "masters." The new ideology not only conceals the domination and exploitation of the poor but also seeks to become a substitute for their own ideological creation, that is, it attempts to keep the poor silent. As Paulo Freire suggests, "The dependent society is by definition a silent society. Its voice is not an authentic voice, but merely an echo of the voice of the metropolis—in every way, the metropolis speaks, the dependent society listens."[13]

Cultural dependence is clearly expressed in the fields of science and technology. The development of applied and theoretical sciences is as stagnant within the poor nations as is their economy. The United States has become the center for military and industrial research and development as well as the center for training persons in practical sciences. Latin American nations have become consumers of technology and of the corresponding training. The inability of the periphery to achieve a self-sustained scientific and technological development undermines their capacity to achieve cultural authenticity in other realms as well.

> Of the many relevant consequences of cultural denationalization in the scientific-technological sphere, one of the most negative for the concerned society is the gradual loss of functionality, which affects its cultural elite as a national group. The basic functional role of cultural elites—the formulation and interpretation of the beliefs of their culture, according to the requirements of the time and the necessities of the concerned society—presents different forms in different socio-historical conditions. . . . Once the demands of economic rationalization are only marginally addressed to the national elite, because the fundamental scientific and technological know-how and expertise are supplied from abroad, the cultural elite loses its economic functionality. This brings about the deterioration of its other roles such as the formulation and administration, in the political plane, of the criteria of legitimacy, and in the social plane, of the criteria of respectability.[14]

Latin American universities become themselves subsidiaries of North American and European schools. Faculty members are trained within the metropolis, funding for programs comes from outside the country, and the curricula echo what is done within metropolitan universities. There is little room for autonomous research, making the intellectual elite merely transmitters of foreign culture and know-how or merely gatherers of data for the research interests of the metropolis.

Many Latin American students and professionals prefer to remain in or return to the metropolis where they enjoy the research facilities and the opportunities to continue to advance intellectually and be able to work under more desirable circumstances than those back home. Even when they return to their homelands, their professional and personal interests are best served by working with the transnational companies.

Ideological domination also expresses itself through the control and influence transnationals have over the means of mass communication that shape public opinion and influence political attitudes. Advertising is at the heart of the survival of newspapers, radio, and television. Most of their income derives from the transnationals. Whoever controls the means of advertising has a great deal of influence over the means of mass communication. Most advertising agencies are foreign-owned or controlled. Decisions concerning who will get their business are made on political as well as business grounds.

Economic stagnation and underdevelopment in general make Latin America's social and political life very unstable. This instability creates conditions for the military establishment to take control over the state and political life. The military, which by and large is composed of individuals from the middle class with a corresponding ideological formation and technical education, is presently one of the principal social and political forces. In spite of its apparent autonomy and independence, the military elite has proven to be a dependent class. It depends on the United States for arms, in particular for advanced weapons, military technology, and organization. This has given the United States a voice in the military policies of these nations. The defense of Christian Western civilization together with a strong anti-Communist attitude has become their common ideology. The defense system of Latin American nations has been integrated into the security needs of the United States. Even Helio Jaguaribe, who has faith in this class' capacity to lead Latin American nations toward a self-sustained process of growth, recognizes that at present the policies they enact enhance the dependence of their nations.

Nationally, the military has developed its own ideology to justify its control: the national security state. Under this ideology, all forms of social protest by workers, peasants, or students to vindicate their rights are denounced as part of the inter-

national Communist movement to undermine and destroy
Western Christian civilization. On the basis of the fear of
Communism, they are able to justify the undermining of civilian governments. This has resulted in polarizing political violence and/or the destruction of political life. What is more
significant, this ideology attempts to conceal some of the real
abuses committed against workers and peasants by disregarding the actual causes of their oppression, diverting attention
instead to the Communist threat. Further, it reduces all conflicts to the East-West conflict, disregarding the conflicts that
take place on the North-South axis, which is the central one.

In short, the international metropolis-satellite structure
perpetuates the position of subordination and the state of domination of Latin American nations. They become "object societies," nations acted upon by their metropolitan centers,
manipulated in their economic, political, and cultural life. This
structure has led to an increased denationalization of wealth
and power and a loss of their capacity to determine themselves.
Although they have been members of the international capitalist system since its beginning, they have not received in propor-
tion to the contribution they have made to the expansion and
consolidation of this economic system. They have remained
marginal to the centers of decision making which give the system its direction. Thus, they have become marginal to the determination of their own political destiny.

## Intracolonialism

Capitalist expansion has been so pervasive that it re-
produces the structure of dependence in the midst of the poor
nation itself. The unequal and combined character of capitalist
development at the international level is reproduced within the
poor nation. At this level too, one sees the outflow of capital and
human talent moving from the rural areas toward the industrial
sectors.

The urban centers of the poor nations function as a mi-
crometropolis in relation to the rural areas. They are the centers of economic activity, cultural activity, and political decision

making. The organization of society as a whole is very much determined in this area. The urban center becomes the medium through which the most backward regions of the nation are connected to the metropolitan centers outside of the country. They enable and make it easy for capital to move from the periphery to the hegemonic center and enable capitalism to become the all-pervasive world economic system.

Nevertheless the poor nations' state of dependence cannot be understood by looking at the economic structure alone. It is indispensable that we look at the role the different social classes that make up society play within it. The economic structure does limit what can be achieved within a given social organization. It even limits the way the society as a whole can be changed. However, the social structure itself is the product of the conscious political policies enacted by the dominant social class. The capacity of the dominant class to persuade and/or coerce other social classes to follow their policies and act according to their value system is vital if the dynamics of the state of dependence and the possibilities for overcoming it are to be grasped.

The internal manifestations of the phenomena of dependence—stagnation and marginality—can only be understood in the context of the dialectics between the prevailing social structure and the policies of dependence enacted by the social classes that rule the nation. Ultimately, dependence is a product of human agency politically organized.

What best describes the internal reality of Latin American nations are the visible signs of underdevelopment itself. Their productive capacity is very low, as is their consumption of socially necessary goods and services. They cannot produce enough goods and services to attend to the needs of their internal markets. As a result, they suffer from an extremely unequal distribution of the goods and services they do have. Their social and political institutions are unstable, incapable of integrating all members of society, and unable to grant all their members a meaningful voice in the determination of their collective destiny.

The Latin American national industrial bourgeoisie, which since 1940 has become the dominant sector of the ruling class, had as its historical project to achieve the industrialization and development of its nations. This social class, however, never achieved the strength and autonomy to play a similar historical role as its European and North American counterpart played. Its dependence on the resources of the agricultural sector to finance the process of industrialization and its need for foreign capital, technology, and organizational skills made it difficult for this class to become a progressive social class, able to strive for a more autonomous development. To achieve the end of more autonomous development it would have had to enact policies that were contradictory to the interests of the agricultural sector and the metropolitan bourgeoisie. It would have had, for example, to regulate foreign investment as well as the exportation of capital and profits. It would have had to give preferential treatment to nationally owned industries, particularly when these were establishing and consolidating themselves. It also would have needed to enact a comprehensive program of land reform, not just a partial distribution of land, that would really have affected the manner of the production of agricultural goods. It would also have been necessary to diversify agricultural production, modernize it in light of the internal needs of the country, and ultimately industrialize it. The success of these policies would have necessitated a broad social mobilization and an alliance with urban workers and peasants who have a real interest in their realization.

The national bourgeoisie proved itself to be a weak, timid, and conservative class. In its view, an alliance with workers and peasants created too much uncertainty. The bourgeoisie was not sure it could control these social classes once they became engaged in a process of revolutionary social transformation. The national bourgeoisie opted for the liberal project and kept its alliances with the agricultural oligarchy and with the metropolitan bourgeoisie intact, both of which continued to secure their own self-interests. These policies were the consolidating factor in the dependence of Latin American nations on the

United States. Thus, they capitulated their historical mission and allowed themselves to be co-opted by the international managerial elite that administers and represents the interests of the transnational corporations.

It is this new managerial elite that has the mission of integrating the various sectors of the ruling class within the periphery: the industrial bourgeoisie, the agro-commercial and agricultural bourgeoisie, the bureaucratic element within the middle class (in particular state bureaucrats), the military establishment, and the wealthier people within the working class who tend to identify their interests with those of the power elite. This new managerial elite must enact policies that attend to the needs of these various sectors of society. When conflicts of interest emerge (and they do emerge), it must arbitrate them.

### Economic, Political, and Cultural Inequalities Between Regions and Social Classes

Economic stagnation is one of the main characteristics of most Latin American nations. The slow process of economic growth experienced by most of these nations is a product of their weak and small internal markets, markets incapable of generating sufficient demand for those goods necessary to achieve a process of self-sustained growth. The policies forwarded by the new managerial elite and enacted by the national bourgeoisie have become an obstacle to the growth and development of the internal market of poor nations. They encourage the intense exploitation of existing markets rather than investing to broaden them. They reinvest capital outside of the poor nation to maximize short-term profits, rather than reinvesting within the country for the sake of long-term development. They have also intensely exploited the current agricultural market rather than attempting to expand and modernize it.

Their capacity to grow is also curtailed by the constant outflow of capital, particularly by the exploitative nature of the productive process. Labor must be exploited to a high degree so it can satisfy the need for profits of both the national and international ruling class. Poor nations develop internally within a framework of a two-level exploitation:

> From the situation of double overexploitation results the excluding character of dependent capitalism under which we live. The economic growth which we witnessed during the 1950s proved it. This growth takes place on the one hand, by incorporating a small sector of the population to the productive system (which, as we saw, is based on overexploitation) and, on the other hand, by excluding and marginalizing ever more extensive sectors of the population.[15]

This double exploitation results in an unequal distribution of wealth. Most members of society have little or no capacity to consume goods other than basic foodstuffs and clothing. Unequal distribution significantly lowers the possibility of social consumption, again reinforcing the difficulties of achieving a level of self-sustained growth and the process of industrialization. Private investors are not encouraged to invest in a market that cannot buy and consume what it produces. Production for local consumption is further curtailed. Poor nations are fitted into an international system of production and consumption in which they provide cheap labor so that others can enjoy the fruits of their work. Within the poor nation, those few people who do have resources to consume cannot sustain a national market. The consumption habits of the economically well off within poor nations reveal that they engage in a form of consumption more suitable to the reality of developed nations. They squander capital resources for their personal gratification, particularly in the consumption of luxury goods. They waste resources for play that others need to survive. This not only drains capital that could be used for the economic growth of the nation but also generates a particular form of consciousness, an indifference to the concrete misery of the poor. Alternatively, the ideology of racial superiority and charges of archaic religions and social values are cited in order to blame the poor for their own misery and powerlessness.

The rural areas are in a position of even greater disadvantage. The agro-commercial and agricultural bourgeoisie is declining in national and international influence. It is more concerned with surviving as an influential class within a more limited realm of influence than attempting to control the nation as a whole. This class still has enough economic and political power within the nation to limit the economic and political influence of both the national industrial bourgeoisie and the transnational managerial elite. However, it is aware that it cannot control the country as a whole and that its own interest is best served and assured by accepting the dominant position of these other social classes. It is aware that the national bourgeoisie and the elites of the transnational corporations prefer to meet their needs rather than deal with the demands of urban and rural workers who represent a more serious threat to their power and privilege.

Rural workers, like their urban counterparts, are subjected to extreme exploitation and dehumanization. Both have problems with job security. Even when they do find work, the threat of losing it causes insecurity, making them tolerate low wages and inhumane working conditions. They perceive their employers as the givers of life and view work itself as a privilege rather than a right. In fact, owners are "lifegivers": they literally do have the power of life and death over workers. Workers are treated not as persons but as productive units. Some workers are treated worse than livestock, and thus they develop a corresponding form of consciousness. Given the way work is structurally organized, it is difficult for workers and peasants to develop class consciousness and become aware of their common problems and interests. Workers sometime perceive each other not as companions but as threats, as the causes of low wages and job insecurity.

Marginality is the other main structural characteristic within Latin American nations. The marginalized are the unemployed, the poor, and the powerless who are structurally kept outside the mainstream of social existence. The marginalized are deprived of having a meaningful voice in the decision-making process by which society determines its destiny. They are deprived of a meaningful voice in the economic and political centers of decision making which affect their lives in a fundamental way. This represents a loss of power that also has implications for the way they partake of the available social goods and services. Hence, the phenomenon of marginality is intrinsically related to that of stagnation. They become an "army of unemployed" which represents a serious social cost and sustains the conditions of political instability. They originate mainly in the rural areas that are unable to absorb the population density and the workforce displaced by the introduction of new technology. The urban center to which this population emigrates cannot absorb it either. This exodus is accompanied by a strong feeling of not belonging. The sociocultural life of the cities remains alien and hostile to the rural population. The personal isolation of these individuals, and the lack of family and support groups, increases their insecurity and loneliness. Conditions emerge for escapist forms of behavior which range from a life of vice to alienated forms of religious expression.

Determining the political preferences and loyalties of the marginalized is extremely difficult. They do not constitute a social class with common interests and visions for society. They are a social group that can be co-opted by a more structurally and ideologically defined class. They can serve as informants to those in power, undermining workers' strikes and students' protests. They can serve as part of a revolutionary movement, either because they can benefit from their involvement in the struggle or because they develop a form of consciousness that makes them loyal to the cause of the poor. They can take a middle-of-the-road option and join traditional populist movements.

An independent workers' political movement and ideology was born when it became clear that the national bourgeoisie was not able to undertake a project of autonomous, nationalist development. Their struggle has intensified social unrest and instability. It has made the vacuum of political authority and legitimacy that exists within Latin American society even more evident. This has led the military to assume greater political control over the workers. In so doing, the problem of political marginality has increased.

More and more, traditional political organizations limit themselves to representing narrow self-interests, making any talk about the common good irrelevant. In the rural areas a clientele type of politics has been predominant. Family loyalties and patronage politics still prevail. If workers and peasants could join forces in a common front, then they could overcome their marginality and recreate space for public life. However, it seems unlikely that such an alliance will take place in the near future. The diversity of their interests, their isolation from each other, and mutual distrust combine to create adverse conditions for them to develop a coherent political option.

At present, the military elite is the only social group capable of preserving the status quo and giving it some semblance of legitimacy. Other sectors of the ruling class have come to appreciate the capacity the military has for preserving some sense of order and peace. It is able to sustain the system of law, and, more importantly, the system of private property. It is also able to resolve and arbitrate the conflicts that emerge within the ruling class. The military, however, has not only achieved peace and order by violating fundamental human rights—in particular the rights of the marginal—but it has also replaced political life with technical expertise.

The inequalities of power and wealth that exist between national regions and social classes is also found in the realm of culture. Illiteracy is extremely high and the amount and quality of education somewhat low. Only the privileged few have access to good schools and the opportunity to study abroad. For the majority, an educational experience consists in becoming functional and integrated into the productive system. It is conformist and does not lead to the creation of a critical consciousness. Educational centers become a means of diffusing the culture and values of the metropolitan society. For the poor and marginal, the cultural lag is such that it is impossible even to transcend their natural and social environment. At this level, oppression is internalized in its crude form and the realm of the "magical" becomes predominant.

## Dependence and the Latin American Church

The church too has been affected by the structure of dependence, in its theological reflection as well as its pastoral work. It has been both partner and victim in the process by which the structure of dependence has consolidated itself. The Latin American church has developed as a dependent church, manifesting the three stages that characterize the socioeconomic experience of dependence of Latin America as a whole.

During the period of conquest and colonization, the church gave unconditional support and even theological rationale to the activities of civil authority. In turn civil authority assisted the church in the process of propagating the faith. Through the legislative process and the organization of the educational system, civil authority responded to the interests of the church. This relationship made the church more and more dependent on the powerful, while at the same time alienating it from the poor and the common people. As Míguez Bonino has noted,

> The Church used the mechanism of civil compulsion, but it depended on the civil authorities and therefore was influenced by their very nature and conditions. When one considers the class organization, which placed in the hands of a few landowning families the total sum of wealth and real authority, it becomes clear that the Church was subordinate, both by its place in the hierarchy of society and by its dependence, to the interests of this group. It is difficult to overestimate the consequences of this fact. . . . It meant that, while the masses became deeply committed to Catholicism, they always felt the official Church as something foreign to them, as a part of "those above" as popular speech calls the small oligarchy who decides their destiny. It meant, finally, that the Church knew no other way of influencing the people—no other pastoral method—than the use of the institutions of society. This use required a good relation with the dominant classes. This decided their attitudes when the first conflicts began to emerge in Latin American society. The colonial Church was tied to a colonial structure.[16]

The church underwent a significant change during the period of the struggles for national independence. The emerging Latin American bourgeoisie understood that it had to break its ties with Spain in order to seek the benefits of new economic ties with England, the new world hegemonic power. Ideologically and religiously speaking, this represented a change from feudalism and Catholicism to libertarianism and Protestantism. The Roman Church saw this change as an attack on the church itself, an undermining of social stability, and a threat to the salvation of the members of society. Fearing the loss of its privileges and social advantages, the church opposed the libertarian movement and opted to support the most conservative sectors of society.

As it became clear that liberalism was an irreversible process, the church's opposition became more theoretical than practical. Practically, the church accommodated itself to the new status quo. In light of shared economic interests the conflicts between libertarian and aristocratic Catholics began to lose importance. As workers began to organize their own independent political organizations and a socialist ideology began to dominate their thinking, liberals and conservatives joined forces to defend the status quo.

The period of the struggles for national independence was also the era of the growth of Latin American Protestantism. The new ruling class saw values and behaviors in this religious expression that agreed with those of liberal capitalism. Even faithful Roman Catholics, who wanted to undermine the power and influence of the church in political life, invited Protestants to organize in their countries. In the early stages, Protestantism was a liberating force. It supported the process of breaking loose from a closed society. Yet, it was unable to preserve its autonomy and independence. It too became a religion of the status quo. It provided religious justification for the libertarian historical project, according to Míguez Bonino:

> The liberal modernizing stage will be then seen for what it was, an ambiguous but necessary moment in our history. Without it, it would have been impossible to break the stranglehold of the

traditional social structure, a barren scholastic philosophy, religious intolerance—in brief, a "closed society." In this perspective, Protestantism will have to be seen in its positive role, both in the religious and in the socio-cultural areas. It offered an interpretation of the Christian faith in which the individual person could be recognized and honored in his or her freedom, his or her capacity for decision and growth, his or her moral responsibility, an interpretation in which society could be experienced, not as a static and closed structure but as a dynamic and reformable process, as a field for the exercise of personal responsibility and social solidarity. It re-claimed for the Christian faith groups of society which the historical changes had uprooted and sent adrift in a modern world for which they were not prepared.

But all these positive contributions should not hide from us other less complimentary features. Protestantism has helped to create a benevolent and idealized image of the colonial powers—mainly of the United States—which disguised the fact of their domination. . . . Protestant communities have been in many cases cultural enclaves which have remained foreign to the life of their countries, unconcerned and indifferent to the needs and problems of the world around them. Institutional dependence and an almost total missionary domination has in many cases kept these churches as little more than appendices of their overseas "headquarters" and fostered a dependent mentality. Their plans and programs have in many cases been merely a reflection or an implementation of the goals, slogans, and programs defined and launched in the United States and, as it was bound to be, they expressed the values, concerns and ideology prevalent in the American Churches, which in turn were closely related to those of the American society as a whole.[17]

After World War II the United States became the new world hegemonic center. Most Protestant churches and missions within Latin America had their headquarters in North America. The mixture of cultural and religious values that this missionary enterprise entailed was soon to emerge with all its synchronistic force.

... there are different and even conflicting influences of the United States in Latin America. This fact is rooted in contradictions within the life of the United States itself. There is a long tradition in America of commitment to freedom, equality, justice, human rights, and education. This tradition has been present in the missionary enterprise from the beginning and is strongly attested in the history of American missions in Latin America and elsewhere. Although it is undoubtedly embodied in the particular characteristics of the society and culture of the United States, it has meant a significant contribution to the life and progress of Latin American countries and a pertinent witness to the liberating power of the Gospel. But the United States has also a strong tradition of imperialistic domination, arbitrary interventions in the life of Latin American countries, abuse of economic and political power, support of the most reactionary and inhuman forces in Latin American countries. These tendencies to arrogance, domination, discrimination, overbearing contempt for the culture and habits of the people in the land have also been present in the missionary enterprise and have meant a counter-testimony.[18]

While Protestantism began its missionary work with the poor, as these early converts emerged and consolidated themselves as the new middle class, so did Protestantism. The poor, who never had an active participation in the liberal capitalist project and whose interest and needs were not included in it, also discovered that they had been abandoned by Protestantism. They found the church insensitive to their struggles for socioeconomic rights and many times saw how it supported the policies of repression by the ruling class. Confronted by the continuous state of misery and powerlessness most Latin Americans were forced to live in, a significant sector of the church began to search for the causes of this oppression, including a scrutiny of the church's own responsibility in sustaining the status quo. As a result, Latin American liberal capitalism began to be perceived more clearly as simply a new, albeit refined way in which the hegemonic center exploited and dominated them.

The Latin American community of faith began to suspect that their thinking and pastoral work reflected the values and experiences of a context quite different from their own. They began to perceive that much of what was regarded as Christian values were in fact the beliefs and practices of a sociocultural context that was not necessarily tied to the faith. They saw how those in power were able to co-opt the faith to propagate their own beliefs and interests. As a result, the sense of justice of the community of faith was awakened. They began to consider the possibility of "a post-colonial and post-neocolonial understanding of the Christian gospel."[19]

Liberation theologians argue that the liberation of the church is intrinsically related to the liberation of the poor nations and the poor social classes within them. The creation of the new church demands that it become actively involved in the social transformation of society. This is the context in which the church can rediscover the particularity of its mission for this part of the world.

Religiously and politically speaking, the term *dependence* as used by liberation theologians seems to be ambiguous. Within our religious tradition the term *dependent* has always had a positive interpretation. In one sense it is necessary and good to rely on others. For the community of faith, religious consciousness consists, among other things, in proclaiming our dependence upon God. To deny our dependence on others, nature, and God can only encourage self-destructive forms of autonomy. Still, even those who make us aware of the positive aspects of dependence recognize that it has moral ambiguities. On the human level, it often leads to relationships of domination and exploitation.[20]

Liberation theologians restrict the use of the term to those cases in which a structural relationship of dependence has emerged. For relationships that lead to mutuality and the realization of the freedom and well-being of the poorest and weakest members of society, they use the term *liberation*. Liberation creates conditions for solidarity and interdependence. It creates conditions for authentic reconciliation because it attempts to overcome those objective and subjective conditions that are obstacles to the concrete realization of mutuality. According to Míguez Bonino,

> solidarity is based on differentiation, on the existence of a real "other" whom I do not absorb into myself or use instrumentally for my own self-realization. We are not dealing here with

merely theoretical propositions; what is at stake is the possibility of real liberation, whether we face the relation of man and woman, education, or the developed countries' relation to the Third World. . . . how can solidarity be really motivated and widened unless there is, at every level of thought and action, the real possibility of openness to "the other."[21]

The term *dependence* can also be translated as "structural violence," which implies the systematic negation of elementary human rights and, thus, of justice.

## Dependence as Structural Violence

Since the Second General Conference of Latin American Bishops at Medillín, Colombia (better known as the Medillín Conference), an inceasing number of Latin American Christians have moved away from a merely descriptive account of the suffering, sickness, and powerlessness that characterize their nations to a more structural and dialectical account of the causes of this inhuman situation. In official church documents and scholarly and popular publications, members of the church hierarchy, organizations of priests, and lay movements have begun to analyze their societies, using the categories, hypotheses, and theories of the sociologists of dependence. They no longer see the situation of dependence as something accidental, fated, or caused by miscalculated, although well-intentioned policies, but as a necessary product of the function of poor nations within the development of world capitalism. Many church members have denounced dependent capitalism as a structure of violence and injustice.

The term *structural violence* is used to describe a social order that by necessity allows the few to appropriate the fruits of the work of the many, thus forming the basis for political instability and powerlessness for most of the people that live within the system. Such a social order makes the use of overt violence a necessary means for preserving and transforming the status quo. A social structure is intrinsically violent when it generates and perpetuates extreme inequalities. José Miranda speaks of it as follows:

No one would say that the workers freely accept the national system of contracts and transactions in virtue of which they are kept in a state of perpetual disempowerment and the capitalists in a perpetual situation of privilege. What forces them to capitulate before the system is the prevailing institutional violence which encircles them with hunger.

Not one ounce of the capital which exists today could have been generated if the workers of our countries had been able to exercise their natural and inalienable right to organize as workers and consumers. Violence prevented them from exercising it, a violence that is institutional, legal, juridical, pseudo-moral, cultural, etc. And thus private ownership continues to be constituted, not only by the means of production, but also of villas, private vacation estates, expensive household furnishings, all the inherited differences which make up social inequality and the classist society.[22]

Laws, traditions, and customs are cited in order to conceal the violent nature of the status quo. The most effective means of giving an appearance of social order and peace is to make the poor accept the present state of affairs as natural. The best way to achieve this is to create a form of consciousness among the poor that excludes the possibility of conceiving a different state of affairs. If they can be persuaded that the security of the present is preferable to the uncertainty and human cost of a different future, then they can be made to accept the way they live as the only human possibility. This condition of hopelessness and fear constitutes the best support for a condition of violence and injustice. It represents a destruction of the human spirit, the core of a person's humanity. Says Míguez Bonino:

In the final analysis, the capitalist form of production as it functions in today's world creates in the dependent countries (perhaps not only in them) a form of human existence characterized by artificiality, selfishness, the inhuman and dehumanizing pursuit of success measured in terms of prestige and money, and the resignation of responsibility for the world and for one's neighbor. This last point is perhaps the most serious. Insofar as this sham culture kills in the people even the awareness of their own condition of dependence and exploitation, it destroys the very core of their humanity: the decision to stand up and become agents of their own history, the will to conceive and realize an authentic historical project.[23]

Liberation theologians argue that those committed to the creation of a more just society cannot avoid participating in some form of political violence. The structure of violence, declares Míguez Bonino, makes it almost impossible to opt for a nonviolent alternative to achieve social change:

> A significant discussion of this issue can therefore be only a discussion on the *violences* and the conditions of violence in our concrete situation. It has to do with who inflicts these different violences and who suffers from them, with the purposes of these different violences, and how these purposes are accomplished (or not) through their use. We must resist all hypostatization of *la violencia,* either to defend it or to attack it. The discussion of violence can only be adjectival of the entire process in movement in Latin America and of the struggle for liberation. Such sentences as "we are against violence wherever it may come from" or "we reject all forms of violence" may be quite "seductive for human and Christian sensibility," as Girardi says but, as he himself goes on to say, they are only hypocritical self-justifications or unconscious cooperation with existing oppressive violence. They can only make sense on the lips of people—who do not usually employ them—who are actively and dangerously involved in the removal of prevalent violence.[24]

The authentic meaning and goal of a revolutionary process is lost if too much emphasis is placed on violence as the revolutionary method. Every authentic revolution aims at the creation of a social order in which the need for violence as a tool for social cohesion will be reduced to a minimum. Even when violence is the only way to open society to new and more humane possibilities, we need to keep in mind that the goal is to "suppress and overcome violence in each and every form it expresses itself."[25] This, in Assmann's view, is the Christian's intention in politics. The use of violence as a tool for social change always brings with it a high human cost and affects those who are the most innocent. What is even more dangerous, it tends to perpetuate itself beyond its reasonable and legitimate need and begins to hurt those it was supposed to serve. Liberation theologians recognize the intrinsic affinity that exists between militant nonviolence and the revolutionary and Christian intention to overcome and suppress all forms of violence. However, they do not believe that the method of militant nonviolence is a viable means of actualizing social change in the present sociohistorical circumstances of Latin American nations. Furthermore, its advocates must recognize its ambiguities and the human cost involved in its utilization. As Míguez Bonino argues,

> Nonviolence has also to ask what is the human cost in lives, suffering, paralyzing frustration, dehumanization, and the introjection of a slave-consciousness. . . . No sentimentalism can replace the sober assessment of the situation. A Christian ethics cannot take refuge in the subjective appeal to "my conscience" or satisfy itself with a readiness to suffer violence without resistance. For it is not our life or comfort as Christians which is at stake—at this point the Christian community can only follow the road of the cross—but the life and humanity of our neighbor. Certainly Christians in the struggle for liberation will witness to their faith—as well as to the ultimate goal of the revolution—by insisting on counting carefully the cost of violence, by fighting against all idolization of destruction and the destructive spirit of hate and revenge, by attempting to humanize the struggle, by keeping in mind that beyond victory there must be reconciliation and construction. But they cannot block through Christian scruples the road clearly indicated by a lucid assessment of the situation. Even less can they play the game of reaction lending support to those who are profiting from present violence or weakening through sentimental pseudo-Christian slogans (however well-meaning) the will among the oppressed to fight for their liberation.[26]

It is morally irresponsible to deal with the issue of the use or nonuse of violence as a tool for social change as a matter of principle and disregard the concrete sociohistorical circumstances in which people find themselves. It is morally irresponsible to deal with such a problem by means of deductive reasoning, seeking to derive from a priori established truths of morality the best means for social change. In the context of the reality of institutional violence, we should recognize that not all forms of violence are the same; not all parties or social classes are equally responsible for its existence. Those forms of violence used systematically to deny the realization of fundamental human rights are qualitatively different from those forms of violence used to open an unjust system so that it makes concrete and visible the rights of freedom and well-being to which all persons as persons are entitled.

No social revolution—a radical transformation of the socio-economic structure and the distribution of power—has ever been achieved in which violence has not played a significant role. Assmann claims that the nonviolent alternative can have a role in shaking the status quo but not in bringing forth its complete abrogation. It can encourage peace, but it is not clear how it can bring about the radical transformation of society that justice demands.

Within the poor nations today, the commitment to free the poor from unjust conditions is the locus from which we judge ourselves as being for or against human dignity. Outside of this commitment, all claims for the defense of human dignity are suspected of being ideological justifications of the status quo. Evolutionary social change is seen by many as the only way to keep life human. However, counters Míguez Bonino,

> as a Latin American Christian I am convinced—with many other Latin Americans who have tried to understand the situation of our people and to place it in world perspective—that revolutionary action aimed at changing the basic economic, political, social and cultural structures and conditions of life is imperative today in the world. Ours is not a time for mere development, rearranging or correction, but for basic and revolutionary change (which ought not to be equated necessarily with violence). The possibility for human life to remain human on our planet hangs on our ability to effect this change.[27]

If liberation theologians are suspicious of those who in the name of human dignity remain passive before the reality of misery and powerlessness that surrounds them, then they are equally suspicious of those who in the name of human dignity find it easy to engage in revolutionary action and believe the use of violence will bring a quick solution to the problems they confront. In their view, the objective and subjective conditions

necessary to overcome the reality of dependence and cultural
violence in Latin America do not yet exist. At present, one can
only conceive a long-term struggle.

Finally, the term *structural violence* refers to the socioeconomic and political relationships that exist between poor nations and the now developed nations. The violence which
characterizes the life of poor nations is only a microcosm of the
violence which prevails in the macrocosm of the world capitalist system. At the international level, we find the same economic, political, and cultural domination and exploitation
which constitutes a continual violation of fundamental human
rights, in this case, the collective right to freedom and well-
being of the poor nations of the Third World. As Gutiérrez says,
"The 'poor' today are the oppressed, those despoiled by the
powerful, the proletariat fighting for the most elementary
rights, the exploited peasant class, the country fighting for its
freedom."[28] At these three levels, the term *structural violence*
is intrinsically related to the issue of social justice.

Thus, Gutiérrez notices favorably how at the meeting in
Puebla, Mexico, the Latin American bishops, with the blessing
of the Pope, transformed the term *structural violence,* which
had become so controversial after Medillín, into the term *institutional injustice* and stressed how such a structure constitutes
a permanent violation of human dignity, particularly for the
poor, a situation of oppression and repression, of increased
pauperization and marginalization of the poor.

For the theologians of liberation, the language of dependence, structural violence, and social injustice are one and the
same. To struggle to transform the structures of dependence is
to significantly reduce the need for violence as a tool of social
cohesion and to create a more just social order. When Gutiérrez, agreeing with André Gunder Frank, claims that the
term *dependence* is "definitely nothing more than a euphe-
mism for oppression, injustice, and alienation," he is expressing
a view shared by most theologians of liberation and the social
theorists of dependence. For all these authors, "The concerns
of the so-called Third World countries revolve around the social

injustice-justice axis, or, in concrete terms, the oppression-liberation axis."[29] This is the axis that defines the sociohistorical coordinates of Latin America today.

The theory of dependence and the concept of structural violence provide the descriptive and evaluative dimensions liberation theologians have of their social reality, revealing how central the issue of social justice is for them. They also reveal the scope of concerns and problems liberation theologians include under the concept of social justice.

Liberation theologians understand the struggle for social justice as one of liberation, that is, in the context of a social revolution. Reforms of the present state of affairs will not do. Thus what they present is an alternative social order with its corresponding concept of justice. Their struggle is one that makes explicit the reality that the opposing camps simply do not have the same fundamental concept of justice, or the same basic concept of the nature of society.

Liberation theologians are primarily, although not exclusively, concerned with questions of social justice more than with those of justice in general. Questions of legal justice—dealing with the punishment of wrongdoing, compensation for injury, fair trial, and right of appeal—are not of their immediate interest. Hence, they do not deal with them in any exhaustive manner. They do, however, express some ideas about the justice of the law or its legitimacy. The topics they deal with explicitly and implicitly have to do with the distribution of socioeconomic goods and services, property relations, the determination of wages, protection and the concrete realization of human rights. They are also concerned with issues having to do with political justice, the meaning and realization of democracy, the legitimate basis of authority, and the distribution of social and political power.

Political justice is intrinsically related to social justice, since how the power of our main social and political centers of decision making is distributed determines, to a great extent, how other forms of distribution will take place. Thus, our right to freedom is integral to our right to well-being. Furthermore, the distribution of goods and services, as well as of power, enables the realization of those intangible goods that give justice its raison d'être: the overcoming of alienation, a sense of worth and respect for self and others, and the possibility for self-realization.

Finally, liberation theologians see an international dimension as an essential part of any authentic and complete consideration of social justice. Contrary to John Rawls, liberation theologians do not believe that questions of justice can be limited to the nation-state. They feel it is unjustified and arbitrary not to ask questions about the relationship between the present wealth and development of today's industrial nations and the poverty and underdevelopment of the nations of the Third World. Questions must be raised as to whether the economic growth that gives the rich nations of the world the necessary stability to allow their citizens greater freedom and well-being is itself the product of an unjust state of affairs at the international realm. Can the absolute value given to the principle of freedom, or at least the unconditional priority given to it, be based on a situation of international exploitation and domination? Is the possibility of justice in the rich nations of the world similar to that of the Greek city state: based on the need to keep the majority of those who live under the system in a condition of slavery?

Liberation theologians argue that there is a dialectical relationship between the struggle for justice in which the poor of their nations are engaged and the international struggle to eliminate their nations' economic and political dependence on the metropolitan center. One form of liberation cannot be fully achieved without the other. Only economic independence from the metropolitan center—which is not the same as economic isolation—will create conditions for the complete exercise of political sovereignty. Thus, freedom from external dependence remains a necessary condition for the creation of a just society both in the poor and rich nations.

## SECOND LEVEL:
## Historico-utopian Liberation

The first level presents us with a radical denunciation of the historical project of liberal capitalism. This historical project that enabled many North Atlantic nations to achieve a high level of development and a system of rough justice has come to represent, for most Latin American nations, a refined way of domination and exploitation. Every denunciation of a historical project presupposes a vision, no matter how imprecise, of an alternative way in which society ought to be organized. This "oughtness" is the concern of the historico-utopian level of liberation. It is at this level that liberation theologians present their views of the new society and of the new person that give the struggle for justice its raison d'être.

Utopian thinking in a liberation perspective is neither wishful nor illusory thinking. It is that form of creative and imaginative thinking that refuses to adapt itself to the logic and the limits of the status quo. It is informed by the social sciences and thus has some sense of how a given social organization works and what possibilities can emerge within it. It seeks to understand "what is" for the sake of bringing about its untested possibilities. It understands every social configuration of power as capable of being rearranged in ways that enable those left at the margin to gain a more significant say in the determination of their destiny. It continually projects reality into what it ought to be and can be.

From a liberation perspective utopian thinking is integral to the rationality of the poor and oppressed and their efforts to overcome oppression. Utopian thinking relevant to the struggle for social justice feeds itself on the experiences that emerge from the praxis of justice. It rejects ahistorical and uncommitted forms of rationality and utopia, denouncing them as alienating and idealistic.

The second level places the struggle for justice within the wider, more complex, and conflictual realm of history. It warns us against the dangers of activism and immediacy. The latter makes us aware that since the struggle for justice takes place in the morally ambiguous political realm, no immediate magical transformation of the present state of affairs is possible. Rather, justice is a long-term and cumulative struggle. The warning against activism makes us aware of the need to keep our ultimate ends and values in mind as we struggle and not to compromise them for the sake of short-term gains. That is, we should not give up the goal of creating a society in which domination and exploitation are significantly reduced for the sake of achieving a better distribution of wealth and power for a small sector of society. The creation of a just society within the Latin American context will be the result of nothing less than a long-term and disciplined commitment to the poor.

## Democratic Socialism

The denunciation of liberal capitalism becomes the annunciation of the consolidation of a new historical project by the poor: democratic socialism. The new social order must be socialist in nature or one that is resolutely moving toward the socialization of the main means of work and centers of power that affect the lives of citizens in a fundamental way. The new society gives priority to the satisfaction of the needs of its people, particularly those worse off; it attempts to create objective and subjective conditions to empower people to become responsible historical actors. This simultaneous quest to realize the rights of well-being and the right to freedom distinguishes this utopian historical project from other major revolutionary movements. Hugo Assmann declares:

> The revolution of the Third World surpasses, in its structure of ideals, both the bourgeois revolution of 1789 and its by-products and the proletarian revolution of 1917 in Russia, because this Third World revolution, taking place in the context of the technological victory of political and economic power at a world scale, incorporates in itself both the struggle for the obtainment of those goods necessary for life with dignity

and the struggle for the freedom to participate at all levels
of social decision making. It is simultaneously an anti-imperial-
istic (anti-oligarchy at the national level) and antitechnocratic
revolution.[30]

It must be an indigenous socialism responsive to the particular historical circumstances of each country, must solve the
concrete contradictions a particular society confronts, and must
build on the socioeconomic and political achievements that
country has already obtained. Thus, there cannot but be a plurality of views of what constitutes socialism and a plurality of
ways of bringing it about.

Liberation theologians assume that significant social
changes within the socioeconomic and political structures of
society have consequences on who we become as persons, i.e.,
for the formation of our characters. The communities we belong to have a determining influence in shaping who we are.
They structure our behavior and reinforce beliefs and value
systems. There is no such thing as a fixed human nature. Persons
cannot be defined as being egoistic or altruistic by nature. By
nature people are not driven by the uncontrollable desire for
social gain nor by the saintly virtue of self-sacrifice. Selfishness,
egoism, the unrestrained desire to acquire and accumulate or
consume are characteristics all persons share in different de-
grees as are the virtues of caring and feeling for others. These
are practices, however, that a given social system encourages or
discourages. People can change. The possibility of changing is
very much determined by changes within the social order.

At the same time they reject all mechanistic interpretations of social change. Persons are not merely the product of
their social environment, just as their social environment is not
merely the sum of individual transactions that take place within
society. Social change by itself does not create a new person, in
the same way that transforming persons does not automatically
induce a new social order. The creation of a new person and a
new social order takes place within a dialectical interaction. Along with the struggle to create a new state of affairs,
a premeditated effort to transform the interpersonal and

even the more intimate inner being of persons must occur.

An unjust social order can distort a person's character and turn his or her creative potentialities into instruments of domination and oppression. Theologically speaking, an unjust social order alienates and distorts our relationships with others and with nature. A just social order, on the other hand, continues and builds on God's creative purpose. To quote Gutiérrez:

> Man fulfills himself only by transforming nature and thus entering into relationships with other men. Only in this way does he come to a full consciousness of himself as the subject of creative freedom which is realized through work. The exploitation and injustice implicit in poverty make work into something servile and dehumanizing. Alienated work instead of liberating man, enslaves him even more. . . .
>
> . . . when we assert that man fulfills himself by continuing the work of creation by means of his labor, we are saying that he places himself, by this very fact, within an all-embracing salvific process. To work, to transform this world, is to become a man and to build the human community; it is also to save. Likewise, to struggle against misery and exploitation and to build a just society is already to be part of the saving action, which is moving towards its complete fulfillment.[31]

The new socialist order must be highly participatory and must democratize not only political life but also economic life. People must have some control in all centers of decision making and at all levels of life that affect them in a fundamental way. Reflective and active participation in the determination of one's collective or national destiny is an integral part of our becoming responsible social agents. Persons constitute themselves as persons not only in the process of dominating nature but also and mainly in the process of creating a more humane and just world. In Gutiérrez's words, "The most important presence of man in history is the struggle to construct a just and fraternal society, where people can live with dignity and be agents of their own destiny."[32]

As far as conditions permit, the values that are to characterize the new society must be intrinsic to the process of bringing it about. The democratic principle, the practice of solidarity, witnessing concretely to the equal consideration and respect due to persons as persons must be present within the process itself of bringing the new social order about. According to Míguez Bonino, justice demands that one reject "all opportunistic action . . . in which the revolutionary intention does not impregnate the strategy and tactics at every point."[33] Revolutionaries have to care for the qualities of actions which seek to bring about the future society.

Thus it is essential, that the poor actively participate in the conception and realization of this historical project from the beginning. A just social order cannot be created for the poor nor can it be created without them. It needs their active participation at all levels of the struggle and our committed solidarity with them.

Economic well-being and political power must go hand in hand with the reappropriation of social symbols and structures of meaning and the creation of a critical consciousness. The struggle for social justice begins precisely when the poor acquire a new consciousness of their social reality. It begins with the realization that existing inequalities are structural and that they can be changed. Such social awareness is not sui generis. It must be cultivated carefully and consistently. The poor, who have internalized the value system of their oppressors, must develop a positive vision of themselves as worthy of equal respect and as capable of responsible social action. They must rid themselves of fatalistic visions of society that ultimately perpetuate the unjust state of affairs. This fatalistic vision of reality, the notion that nothing can or will change in any significant way, is usually accompanied by a sense of powerlessness, apathy, and lack of class solidarity.

Paulo Freire's *Pedagogy of the Oppressed* provides liberation theologians with an instrument to raise the critical consciousness of workers and peasants who have been subjected to extreme forms of exploitation and domination. His pedagogical method is congruent with that of liberation theologians. It assumes a preferential option for the poor and intends to create in them a critical consciousness. It is based on the principles of democracy and encourages a sense of solidarity, community, and the worth and equal regard due to all persons. These are key virtues that make us aware of the value of the procedural elements of justice but also give the quest for justice a precise end, i.e., the liberation of the poor. In this sense it can be argued that Freire's pedagogical method is a pedagogy of justice.

Since no one can escape the oppressive modes of consciousness created by the present unjust state of affairs, it is necessary for all who participate in the struggle for a new social order to participate in some form of liberating pedagogy. This is particularly true for those who, not being poor themselves, must be educated to understand the world and expectations of the poor. They are very likely to discover how they have participated in the ideology of domination. They too must learn how to become persons of the Third World.

The new socialist order must awaken persons to recognize their communal or social nature. The individualistic understanding of human society must be transformed into a more relational and social view of individuality. Our vision of society must be transformed from an instrumental concept of the social—society as the place from which we derive necessary goods and services—to a more substantive notion of the social—society as part of what it means to live a life worthy of the name *human.* Persons must regain a sense of the common good different from that of bourgeois society, which identifies the common good with the sum of what the individuals within society claim is good for them. We must begin to regain the sense that social life itself demands from us—that we be faithful to the relationships that sustain it.

For all the goodness implied in social existence, liberation theologians do not claim that socialism is an end in itself. The ultimate criterion for social justice is a society's capacity to provide for the life needs of all those who live within it. Even the most revolutionary society is evaluated on the basis of its capacity to attend to the needs of freedom and well-being of all its members, in particular, those of the poor.

These criteria also provide a limit as to the way persons can be treated. While socialism deprives capitalists of their capacity to exploit and dominate others, it cannot deprive them of making a living and having a meaningful political voice. To deprive them of these rights, there must be overriding reasons. Without being simple-minded about this, liberation theologians argue that the liberation of the oppressed and the liberation of their oppressors go hand in hand. The character of the new social order will be affected by the way the former oppressors are treated.

## The New Person

The ultimate end of the struggle for liberation is the creation of a new person. The distribution of wealth and power are meaningful in that they create conditions for the emergence of a new person. "It is important to keep in mind that behind—or rather, through—the struggle against misery, injustice, and exploitation the goal is the *creation of a new man,*" according to Gutiérrez.[34] This is the motivating idea behind the struggle. Still, says Assmann, the new person does not "emerge as a spontaneous product of social structures, although these structures necessarily are the material conditions of his birth as a new man."[35] The new person emerges as a result of intense struggle with the tensions found in nature and society; that in itself is a process of liberation.

The new person can be defined as a *being of praxis,* one who is capable of critical reflection and responsible action and of placing "the common good before his own individual interest," a being who is shaped by solidarity and creativity, over against "the individualistic distorted humanity of the present system."[36] This is a person inclined to serve others, particularly those who are worse off within society. The new person's greatest service is to enable and empower others to become beings of praxis so they too can participate in the process of recreating society so as to enhance justice within the political community.

## The Needs of the Poor, Justice and Human Rights

Within a liberation perspective the poor should hold a privileged position from which to judge social structures and determine policy. Their presence awakens us to the moral imperative to remain committed to the struggle for social justice. This commitment to the poor leads liberation theologians to opt for the criterion of need as the most adequate and relevant consideration in determining questions of the distribution of wealth and power. Need is the criterion that serves as the material content of their notion of justice. Their understanding of human need is fairly broad and comprehensive. They are aware, as Míguez Bonino says, that the idea of need "can, to be sure, be misinterpreted in a narrow sense as limiting history to man's effort to find food and shelter, but it need not be so if 'need' is seen in terms of man's total experience."[37] Under the category of need they include all that a person lacks to become a person capable of participating in as many aspects of their social existence as they choose. Things besides food and shelter, if lacking, will harm the person in a fundamental way, such as the freedom to make significant moral and political choices.

Need, as the criterion for social justice, assumes that persons as persons are equal in morally relevant ways and that they are entitled to equal respect and consideration regarding the justice claims they raise. It seeks to make this equality visible within the socioeconomic realm and the political realm, i.e., it seeks the creation of an egalitarian society. Egalitarianism, while intending to reduce all forms of extreme inequality that have emerged within society, does not seek to impose uniformity and sameness among the members of society. Society requires social differentiation and a complex division of labor. Differences will exist in remuneration for the different tasks performed. Further, as people engage in daily transactions, it becomes impossible to preserve a condition of sameness and radical economic equality among them. People will always have preferences and strive to obtain goods and services that others have no desire for. Inequalities are, for the most part, based on natural differences and the options we make to develop some of our talents, usually at the expense of other gifts. It would indeed be unjust to deprive the talented from developing their talents in order to equalize them with the less talented, as it would be unjust and equally oppressive to demand from the less talented that they achieve levels of excellence beyond their capabilities.

Egalitarianism seeks the eradication of those extreme forms of inequality that enable some to dominate and exploit others. Inequalities that do not entail domination are not to be eliminated. As long as all members of society are able to achieve the level of well-being of which they are capable, there is no reason to eliminate those inequalities of wealth and power that are intrinsic to social existence.

The basic and fundamental human needs liberation theologians make reference to are the rights to freedom and well-being. The struggle for liberation does not "only aspire to obtain material goods for all, but also their active participation at all levels of life."[38] To deprive persons of these rights is to harm people in a fundamental way. It is to deprive them of what they need to become beings of praxis. These rights are not only means for the realization of one's potentialities but are very much part of what it means to be human.

The right to freedom is embodied in the political and civil rights people must have in order to participate in the determination of their individual and collective destiny. It guarantees no impediments to one's effective political participation such as fear, coercion, lack of relevant information, and the inability to assemble to discuss and make public one's political views. It also honors one's participation in the main centers of decision making within society: to run for office, to express political consent on a regular basis, and to voice public criticism. The right to well-being requires those socioeconomic goods and services such as work, housing, health care, and education, all of which guarantee the right to live as well as our capacity to sustain life.

From a liberation perspective the function and duty of the state is to see that those members of society who are unable to obtain these rights have access to them. Given the present socioeconomic conditions of Latin American nations, it is a matter of priority that the state provide the masses with what they need to live. The goods and services guaranteed by the right to well-being must be given priority. This provides the context for the concrete realization of the right to freedom. Both the right to freedom and the right to well-being are equally important; neither is merely a means to secure the other. Rather, the realization of one necessitates the realization of the other. One can never assume that by safeguarding one the other is automatically assured. Still, the reality of extreme misery and powerlessness under which most Latin Americans live makes liberation theologians give priority to the right to well-being. From their perspective we have not reached the sociohistorical conditions to reverse the order of priority. According to Hugo Assmann,

> an alternative understanding of human rights has to break with the classical indistinctness—which sees all human rights as equally important so that when one is affected all are equally affected—that has characterized bourgeois juridical ideology (all men are equal before the law, etc.). Only by giving priority to those rights—as guaranteed and not merely ideal rights—that affect more directly the integrity of life and the means of life (physical integrity, food, health, shelter, education), and only by subordinating all other rights to the need of preserving these more fundamental ones, is it possible to have a more historical definition of the basis of the concept of "liberty." Every abstract conception of individual liberty, given priority over the preservation of the fundamental rights to life and of the means of life, lends itself to the emptiness of meaning of the liberal understanding of human rights, rights which anyhow have been systematically denied to most of humanity. The need to subordinate some rights to others considered more basic or fundamental is one of the most difficult things to accept, even by persons who are open-minded and relatively progressive. It is a block that one frequently confronts. "Freedom of thought, of conscience and expression" is for many the frame of reference from which to define liberty, not the need for food, health, shelter, physical integrity. For many it seems, all attempts against a person's physical integrity (torture for example) are horrible because they attempt against freedom of conscience and not because it is an attempt against a person's material life. The fact that this internalized bourgeois ideology that inverts the priorities might be the explanation of the enormous power that bourgeois ideology has of "coopting" and

"integrating" a language that—without the guarantee provided by this blockage—would be dangerous to it. President Carter in his speeches and the Trilateral Commission in their studies, thus, feel free to speak of "fundamental human rights," "basic necessities," and even make use of the same example already mentioned. But in their context these are merely empty linguistic signs. In our view only a praxiological tie to the concept of the priority of rights, that is, the transformation of the ideal into an efficient and guaranteed right, will assure us that the verbalized priority be made truth.[39]

The rights to freedom and well-being are normative. They are moral properties all persons should have. They place limits upon the way society and others can treat us, and they entitle all to make certain claims against others and society as a whole. They are not a matter of social convention, nor can society merely give them and take them away as it pleases or finds advantageous. The protection of these rights ultimately gives the social order and the system of laws that regulates it its moral legitimacy and authority. When a social order systematically violates these rights, it becomes obligatory as a matter of justice to engage in social change. "To a right recognized in principle many times there is no possibility of defending it in practice: it is at this time that we must make a concrete and determinative moral decision."[40] These are times when revolutionary praxis can be justified.

Since human rights are not the rights of the egoistic person, they are not to be understood in a narrow individualistic way. They are moral properties that defend not only the interests of the self but also the equally legitimate interests of others and of society as a whole. Within a liberation perspective, those who enjoy the rights of freedom and well-being are under obligation to assist others to obtain them as well. Quoting Dietrich Bonhoeffer, Gutiérrez argues:

"freedom is not something man has for himself but something he has for others. . . . It is not a possession, a presence, an object, . . . but a relationship and nothing else. . . . Being free means 'being free for the other,' because the other has bound me to him. Only in relationship with the other am I free." The freedom to which we are called presupposes the going out of one-self, the breaking down of our selfishness and of all the struc-tures that support our selfishness; the foundation of this freedom is openness to others.[41]

Such acts of self-giving create conditions for mutuality; authen-tic self-giving calls for a response and usually gets one. Self-giving is not an act of surrendering to the other and subjecting oneself to his or her exploitation and domination. Rather, it is an attempt to create community for the sake of mutual self-realization. A being of praxis has the moral quality of endurance in the quest for mutuality.

Socialism provides as a new historical project the possibility of making the fulfillment of the rights to freedom and well-being accessible to all members of society. It will not bring the eradication of all conflicts and disagreements that are intrinsic to social life. Yet, it does represent a greater good that should not be considered irrelevant nor meaningless. Quoting a group of priests from Chile, Gutiérrez claims that:

> Socialism, although it does not deliver man from injustices caused by personal attitudes nor from the ambiguity inherent in all systems, does offer a fundamental equality of opportunity. Through a change in the relationships of production, it dignifies labor so that the worker, while humanizing nature, becomes more of a person. It offers a possibility for the even develop-ment of the country for the benefit of all, especially the most neglected. It asserts that the motivation of morality and social solidarity is of higher value than that of individual interest, etc. ... All this can be implemented if together with the transforma-tion of the economic structure, the transformation of man is undertaken with equal enthusiasm. We do not believe man will automatically become less selfish, but we do maintain that where a socio-economic foundation for equality has been estab-lished, it is more possible to work realistically toward human solidarity than it is in a society torn asunder by inequity.[42]

At present the defense of human rights has to be under-stood as the defense of the rights of poor nations and the poor social classes within them. The language of rights must be freed from the ideological use the rich and powerful make of it. It will then become clear that the quest for human rights cannot be

limited to the assurance of civil and political rights. Priority
must be given to the right to well-being or to the right to life.
The basic equality that must be achieved is socioeconomic
equality. Justice is more than the protection of political rights;
it is also the empowerment of the weak so they can concretely
exercise these rights. Democracy for the poor is more than the
right to vote; it is also the right to participate in the decision-
making process in the economic realm.

One's active involvement within the class struggle on the
side of the poor is the context from which one can speak meaningfully of justice and human rights. All talk of justice, social
reconciliation, the common good, and peace that does "not take
into account the deep causes of present conditions and the real
prerequisite of building a just society [is] merely escapist."[43] All
of these terms express the innermost longings of most of humanity but their concrete realization demands that we engage
in a struggle to overcome the objective and subjective conditions that make their realization impossible. It is necessary to
overcome the inequalities that keep people separated from and
suspicious of one another. While for those in power the class
struggle is an occasion to dominate and exploit the poor, for the
poor, the class struggle represents an occasion to create a society beyond the oppressor/oppressed axis.

### THIRD LEVEL:
## Faith and Liberation

The ultimate meaning of the struggle for social justice is
unveiled at the level of faith, the religious dimension. For liberation theologians, the creation of a more just state of affairs is
an intrinsic part of our response to that personal God who acts
in history: "The struggle for social justice is in its own right very
much a part of salvation history."[44] This conviction in a God
who can make a historical difference and who enables us to
explore new possibilities within history sustains many Christians commited to the struggle for liberation. I will now examine some of the theological themes that disclose shades of
meaning in the struggle for social justice.

## Sin

From a liberation perspective, sin is not only an individual, personal, and inward or spiritual fault but also a material, collective, and sociostructural phenomenon. Liberation theologians concern themselves with the reality of sinfulness not in its pure or disembodied form, the general condition of sinfulness in which all humans share, but as it becomes manifest in specific or concrete forms. Gutiérrez declares:

> In the liberation approach sin is not considered as an individual, private, or merely interior reality—asserted just enough to necessitate a "spiritual" redemption which does not challenge the order in which we live. Sin is regarded as a social, historical fact, the absence of brotherhood and love in relationships among men, the breach of friendship with God and with other men, and, therefore, an interior, personal fracture. . . . Sin is evident in oppressive structures, in the exploitation of man by man, in the domination and slavery of peoples, races, and social classes. Sin appears, therefore, as the fundamental alienation, the root of a situation of injustice and exploitation. It cannot be encountered in itself, but only in concrete instances, in particular alienations.[45]

Collective sin also represents a fixation upon self, an act of disregard for the other in need. It is a negation of that God who is self-revealed as one who constantly emerges from self-containment and serves those in need, regardless of whether they are deserving or not. A society that negates life for those who live in it manifests itself as a sinful society. Dependence can be properly interpreted as a situation of sinfulness in part because it is an unjust situation that "does not happen by chance, it is not something branded by a fatal destiny: there is human responsibility behind it."[46] It is possible to argue that the rich and powerful have greater responsibility since they determine policies and do so because it benefits them. They struggle very hard to keep things as they are. The poor and powerless, however, are also responsible insofar as they tolerate and remain complacent with the status quo. Ultimately, sinfulness goes much deeper than class distinctions. According to Míguez Bonino,

No human group or class can be made the exclusive and definitive bearer of evil in history. Evil is a solidary and total responsibility of mankind, and if it is true that it finds
historical embodiment within specific conditions and that a
class or a nation can be the typical and dominant representative of it at a certain point in history, it is also true that it
cannot erase the power of the risen Christ present in all humanity.[47]

We can never overcome our sinful condition, but we can
and are called to overcome particular manifestations of human
sinfulness. The universal and all-embracing character of sin
does not make it impossible for humanity to improve its life in
new and unexpected ways. God provides conditions for humanity to strive for the greater good rather than merely conform
to the lesser evil. We are called to conversion, a conversion
that has a social dimension. It demands our commitment
to the creation of a more just world. We are not liberated
from sin through the act of conversion, but we are liberated to make a historical difference as witnesses of God's kingdom.

The fullness of the liberation men and women long for
demands the eradication of the reality of sinfulness, the root
cause of all injustice. From this religious perspective, it becomes
clear that women and men cannot by themselves achieve the
fullness of liberation. History is not self-redemptive, although
redemption takes place historically. The present unjust state of
affairs has "deeper roots than the distortions of the capitalist
society"[48] so much so that "a social transformation, no matter
how radical it may be, does not automatically achieve the suppression of all evils."[49] No matter how radically the social order
is transformed, those realities which make questions of justice
necessary will always emerge. Men and women cannot reestab-
lish, by their own efforts, the bonds of solidarity they have
broken with each other and with God.

The fullness of liberation is nothing but a free gift. The
actualization of justice and the opportunity to experience new
ways of being a person have at their foundation the reality of
the gift of grace.

## God and Jesus

Liberation theologians have a strong concept of the presence of God within history. The deity is thoroughly historical, not because God comes from history, but because history comes from God. The God of Scripture is a passionate, caring God, very much concerned with the well-being of all of creation. We encounter God in our commitment to forward the freedom and well-being of humanity. To experience God as the enabler of new possibilities as well as the sustainer of what forwards life is a privilege. God calls us to submerge ourselves in the historical processes and seek to transform the status quo. God is one radically committed to human justice.

> The injustice, the mercilessness, the oppression, and the exploitation to which all cultures have learned to resign themselves are precisely what Yahweh wants to abolish in the world. The great purpose of God's intervention in human history is definitively to eliminate all this injustice and enmity which many Christians, it would appear, find so normal.[50]

God has revealed a divine preferential option for the poor and their struggles. Through them, God calls us to rethink and redirect our pastoral work and our theological reflection. The community of faith is being summoned "to a new departure in the understanding and obedience of the faith."[51] Our participation within social movements that seek the liberation of the poor becomes a privileged position from which to know God and, what is more important, to be known by God. God is known and found among those who have no one to defend, forward, and protect their well-being and freedom. God dwells among the "weak and the oppressed symbolically expressed through the figures of the stranger, the widow, and the orphan."[52]

The God of Scripture is the liberating God of the Exodus who creates a people where there were no conditions for a community to emerge. God is the prophetic God who demands from people a perpetual disposition to do justice, in particular to the powerless and the poor. God is the Creator, sustainer, and redeemer of life who denounces all forms in which death makes itself manifest. To deprive others of what they need to live and to remain complacent while others struggle to survive is to deny God or to be idolatrous. God suffers whenever humanity is deprived of life. God takes suffering upon Godself and calls us to do the same.

God expects from us much more than acts of sacrifice and spiritual development. God expects from us a life committed to caring for others, both at the personal and political level. Our commitment to justice makes us aware of the fullness of divine love. There is no greater worship to God than the empowering of the weak and powerless.

God's preferential option for the poor is not a denial of divine love for the whole of humanity. The poor are not assured a place in God's kingdom because of the historical accident of their belonging to a given social class under particular sociohistorical circumstances that made them disadvantaged and oppressed. Nor are the poor more virtuous in any morally and religiously significant way. God made the poor chosen ones just because they are poor, in spite of considerations of merit or lack of it. God does justice to the poor solely because they are in need and calls upon God's people to do the same. The question of who is responsible for their poverty is secondary to the issue of what we can do to free them from it. This project enables us to participate in God's historical mission or to work for the well-being of all nations.

The presence of the poor makes us aware that the promise of liberation is still unfulfilled. We cannot sacralize any social order. The poor are the "other," who call us to move beyond ourselves and make a commitment to the well-being of others. They challenge us to become a people of the covenant, pointing us in the direction of social justice. As Gutiérrez has said:

> To be just means to be faithful to the covenant. Faithfulness means justice and it means holiness. Justice in the Bible is a notion which brings together the relationship to the poor and the relationship to God. Only in this way is it synonymous with holiness. To be faithful to the covenant means to practice that

justice which is implied in the action of the God who liberates the oppressed.[53]

Through his life, death, and resurrection, Jesus reveals himself as the Christ, as the one who continues God's saving purpose for humanity by identifying himself with the poor and being committed to the realization of justice for the poor.

> Jesus Christ himself is the new covenant. In him God becomes the Father of all peoples, and all people recognize themselves to be his children and therefore brothers and sisters among themselves. . . . The universality of the New Covenant passes through death and is sealed by the Resurrection. The death of Jesus is a consequence of his struggle for justice, of his proclamation of the kingdom, and of his identification of the poor.[54]

Historically speaking, it is clear that the poor are the ones who have the most to gain from the struggle for liberation. Their concrete liberation, however, has a potentially universal dimension which transcends the narrow and limited nature of the demands, intentions, and achievements of the poor. Their liberation, in spite of themselves, has a universal character that agrees with the universality of God's saving purpose for humanity. Through the liberation of the poor, humanity as a whole experiences a liberating transformation.

Jesus came to proclaim the kingdom of peace and justice that is both present and yet awaits its final fulfillment. He placed his pastoral work within the prophetic tradition, making the praxis of justice constitutive to the act of faith. Christ is the new covenant, a new revelation of what it means to be a disciple of justice.

Jesus reveals not only God's true nature and purpose, but also our innermost authentic selves. He reveals the quality of life proper to the new humanity, a life committed to the reign of peace and justice. Christ makes us aware that we cannot be satisfied with who we are and how we live. Christ calls us to be people for others, so they too can enjoy the promise of fullness of life. We know Jesus comes from God because of his commitment to justice and because of his experience of the victory of life over the powers of death. Jesus takes seriously the misery experienced by the poor and denounces it as sinful. He attends to the needs of those he encounters in his pastoral journey, chooses a life of poverty, and accepts the punishment of a world that denies the poor justice. All of these things enable us to recognize Jesus as being sent by God. Miranda suggests that

> in order for Yahweh to be revealed effectively *in Jesus Christ* the efficacy of the works must be of the same kind as the efficacy of the word, namely, the unmistakable revelation of the God who does not let himself be neutralized, because he is God only in the imperative of justice.[55]

If God and Jesus are mediators empowering persons to persevere in their commitment to bring about the kingdom, then God and Jesus are also mediators who respect the dignity of their creatures. They allow men and women the freedom and space necessary for them to conduct their own affairs. God's promise of the inevitability of the realization of the kingdom does not free humanity of its historical responsibility but rather gives humanity a moral imperative, placing it under the obligation to respond to God's purposes. Between God's act of creation and the ultimate realization of the kingdom, the creative mediation of humanity exists.

God frees God's people from the paralyzing forms of anxiety and fear that are intrinsic to a struggle for justice taken under the most adverse odds. The divine promises make us aware that ultimately no immediate or remote historical power can prevent the final realization of the kingdom of justice. This assurance can free us to make a stand even when we are aware that we are not in control of all the variables and cannot be sure of the final outcome of our actions. This "freedom from" is transformed into a "freedom for," a "more daring hope and intense courage," for a fuller commitment to "the political vocation of transforming the world into a more humane reality."[56] In spite of the temptations to which he was subjected, Jesus never attempted to bring his divine powers to bear in the resolution of the socioeconomic and political problems he confronted and was victimized by. Jesus, too, asserts the autonomy and independence of the sociohistorical realms. These are the realms for the exercise of human responsibility. Jesus rejected the role of messianic political leader. His mediation thus is that of a representative who is neither heteronomous nor autonomous. Míguez Bonino notes that

> . . . the German woman theologian Dorothee Sölle has established a valuable distinction between a "substitute" and a "representative." The former replaces and absorbs the person and initiative of those whom he substitutes, the latter takes up the temporarily necessary function of doing, on behalf of the represented—a minor, an incapacitated, a powerless person or group—that which he or they cannot do, *in order that they may arrive at the point at which they may themselves do it.* He intends to do this in such a way that the represented may be objectively and subjectively empowered. Man has not been cancelled or replaced by Christ: he has been reinstated in a covenant relationship in which he will "grow into full maturity," i.e., grow into the fullness of creativity, freedom, fellowship which Jesus himself displayed and made available. The mediation of Christ is not the substitution of man . . . it is the restitution of man as God's free and active agent in God's humanizing purpose.[57]

God's love toward us manifests itself in God's being for us without violating our dignity as beings of praxis. God's love is a love of solidarity, enabling us to fulfill our historical vocation in free response to the divine will, and empowering us for this task.

## The Kingdom of God

In a number of ways theologians have attempted to establish a relationship between the kingdom of God (the religious realm proper) and the struggle to create a more just society (the realm of morality). Some have argued that the kingdom and the struggle for justice are independent and unrelated realms of human experience. The struggle for justice is seen as a moral/political struggle, to be justified solely on moral/political grounds. The realization of the kingdom is neither enhanced nor threatened by this struggle. The struggle for justice and the liberation of the poor have no ultimate religious significance.

Religion concerns itself with personal salvation, a distinct and unrelated quest from concerns about justice.

Others see no distinction between the kingdom and the struggle for justice. In this perspective, the religious and the moral lose their uniqueness. On the one hand, some people view the struggle for justice as significant only because it is a religious imperative. If it were not for its religious grounding, the struggle for justice would have neither religious nor moral value. Outside the religious there cannot be any kind of moral significance. Morally significant deeds are done exclusively out of respect for God's prior manifestation of love. This is the only morally significant motive. Others, on the other hand, have claimed that religion itself is significant because of its moral content. The symbol of the kingdom is significant because of the moral imperative to struggle for a more just society. While the first alternative sees no dialectical relationship between the kingdom and the struggle for justice, the second alternative attempts to resolve the dialectical tension by reducing either the religious to the moral or the moral to the religious.

From a liberation perspective a permanent dialectical interaction exists between the kingdom and the struggle for social justice. The kingdom and the struggle for justice are different but mutually related. Each has its own integrity and influences the other, but neither is reduced to the other. The theologically significant makes a moral difference; the morally significant is theologically significant as well. Finally, we recognize that theological and religious convictions and beliefs can lead the community of faith to act in ways that transcend what moral reason demands. One example of this is the claim liberation theologians make that justice demands that we attend the needs of the poor solely on the basis that they have a need which we can satisfy.

The creation of a just society is intrinsic to faith and makes a real difference in terms of the final realization of the kingdom. Still the kingdom cannot be identified with any particular historical project and social order, no matter how just it is. The creation of a just society is not a sufficient condition for the realization of the kingdom. The kingdom remains a gift of God. Its realization transcends what is humanly possible.

All historico-political actions that respond to God's care for the poor are intrinsic to the quality of life announced by the kingdom. These actions and events are promised eschatological fulfillment. Still, we must always be aware of the intrinsic ambiguity of every historical achievement. We must always be aware that our justice is not God's justice. What God gives us as a gift transcends all our expectations.

## Love and Justice

Love is the term that best expresses the sociopolitical and historical praxis of Christians. It is the language through which Christians "can articulate their revolutionary intentions."[58] Love cannot be exhausted in the realm of intimacy and privacy. It also has a sociopolitical dimension. It does not remain in the sphere of motivations but also attempts to make a historical difference. This makes justice an intrinsic aspect of Christian love.

José Porfirio Miranda argues that "one of the most disastrous errors in the history of Christianity is to have tried—under the influence of Greek definitions—to differentiate between love and justice."[59] One must come to recognize that, politically speaking, love and justice seek the same results and share the same concerns. Hugo Assmann asserts: "The clear definition and realization of the just interest of the oppressed is the historical embodiment of love."[60] Acts of love and justice have permanence on their side.

Efficacious love seeks to humanize the world and those who live within it. Love is action directed toward the other informed by the needs of the other. It is a gratuitous action, done solely for the sake of the other with the intention of attending his or her needs. Because love is a concern for the well-being of others, in particular the poor, it is "inextricably interwoven with justice."[61] Without this concern for the justice element of love, love would deteriorate into a charitable paternalism that does not call for the creation of a new social reality.

The sense of justice is the only love that truly gets to the heart of the matter. With great intuition Bigo points this out: "The supreme delicacy of charity is to recognize the right of the person being given to"; *because of this recognition, love is love* and not a humiliating paternalism, which because of who knows what mental depravities came to be confused with love, even though we can all see that it is an oppressive insult to the neighbor. Love which is not an acute sense of justice and an authentic suffering-with-my-outraged-brother, such love *does not transcend.* It is satisfied with itself although with its words it denies that it is so; and thus it remains in itself and does not transcend. If it is not equivalent to saying, "You have a complete right to this and I am not condescending to you in any way," then not even the genuine love between man and woman is able to transcend.[62]

In today's world the possibility of effectively attending the needs of the poor demands much more than private acts of charity. To love today demands that we become engaged in transforming praxis seeking to create a more just social order. As Paul Ricoeur notes, true love must be coextensive with justice:

If love is a category of the Kingdom of God and, as such, it implies an eschatological dimension, then it equals justice. We show little or no understanding of love when we make charity the counterpart and supplement of, or the substitute for, justice; love is co-extensive with justice; it is its soul, its impulse, its deep motivation; it lends it its vision, which is the other, the absolute value of which it testifies. . . . At the same time, justice is the efficacious, institutional, and social realization of love.[63]

The neighbor in need today is not just the individual but also collectives, social classes, nations. Love today is necessarily a political activity.

The practice of love takes place within different realms of human existence. In all of them it expresses itself as a concern for the other so that she or he too can achieve the fullness of life. Love takes place within the family, within marriage, and within friendship. Historically and politically speaking, love expresses itself as the attempt to provide fullness of life and the experience of community to the majority of the poor and oppressed who have been kept marginal. Political love does not exhaust the fullness of love, but without it we lose a significant dimension of love that makes all other manifestations of it an incomplete experience.

Our love of God must express itself in all of these levels. We love God through our loving relations with others. True love of God is always mediated through the other, in particular the other in need. For liberation theologians there is a "total material identity between our love for God and our love for the 'non God,' for the other than God, who is our neighbor."[64] However, we must keep in mind that "the neighbor is not an occasion, an instrument for becoming closer to God. . . . love for God is expressed in a true love for man himself."[65]

Love calls for and demands the reunion of all people as a way to enable and sustain their mutual self-realization, freedom, and well-being. The quest for the reunion of humanity is an integral part of the Christian faith because it is a faith centered around the passion of love. It is a faith with a strong sense of the need for community for the realization of persons.

If there is a distinction between love and justice, then it is not a qualitative one but rather one of intensity. To share in the gratuitous love of God is to be freed to become more radically committed to the struggle for social justice. The Christian is given greater freedom to serve the one in need, the freedom to be a new person: "The new man is the man that loves, the one who has been set free for creative existence in service to others."[66] This freedom makes the Christian totally available, that is, available unto death. Says Míguez Bonino:

> The Christian has left his death behind him; to that extent he does not need to make an effort to ensure his own life. There is, therefore, an availability which cannot be limited by the threat that otherwise seems insuperable—death. A Christian can risk his life. Many have done it. . . . Non-Christians have also done it, moved by a love which believers cannot but admire and for which they praise God. What matters here, nevertheless, is to become conscious of the freedom for self-giving available to those who know that "death . . . cannot separate us from the love of Christ."[67]

For Hugo Assmann:

> The distinction between the Christian and the humanist must
> not be sought, of course, in a distinction and separation of
> tasks in the process of humanizing history, but rather in a
> "more" of intensity and criticism in the commitment for lib-
> eration.[68]

It is the concern with human need that makes justice intrinsic
to love. Justice is more than legality and impartiality. In its
social dimensions it is mainly the attempt to liberate the poor.
Míguez Bonino argues that "love operates in this alienated
world by establishing justice. And justice is not measured by
some impartial or legal regulations but by the redressing of the
condition of the weak."[69]

Although liberation theologians emphasize the cost involved in true acts of love within the context of oppression and
domination, they do not understand love solely in terms of
self-sacrifice, for love calls for a loving response. We are called
to persevere in our love toward others, to care for the others'
needs because this creates conditions of mutuality and community. We are called to serve others who are in need merely
because they have needs and we have resources to satisfy them.
This obligation of love-justice does not intend to make us vic-
tims of others' exploitation and domination. One cannot allow
others to take advantage of our love and use it to reverse or
perpetuate a relation of domination. Even acts of self-sacrifice
must take into consideration the question of mutuality, an intrinsic dimension of justice.

While justice is perceived as intrinsic to love, this in no way
implies that the struggle for justice exhausts the totality of love.
There are many more expressions and experiences of love beyond the political. As Jon Sobrino indicates, love is a broader
and more comprehensive category than justice. Still commitment to justice, that dimension of love that calls us to provide
the majority which is poor and oppressed with what they need
to achieve a life worthy of the name human, is necessary for us
to grasp the fullness of God's loving grace.[70]

## The Church

The church itself is testimony that the gift of salvation and the practice of love intrinsic to the life of faith are communal experiences as much as they are individual ones. From a liberation perspective, it is necessary to "break out of a narrow, individualistic viewpoint and see with more Biblical eyes that men are called to meet the Lord insofar as they constitute a community, a people."[71] All efforts to create and sustain community are intrinsic to salvation. For liberation theologians "individualism of salvation is the very negation of the faith of Jesus Christ."[72] Christians are called as a community to engage in the proclamation and realization of the kingdom. This is an intrinsic part of the church's mission to preserve, reinterpret, and proclaim the key symbols, myths, and events that give the church its unique identity.

The church must define the nature of its mission both in light of its interpretation of Scripture and religious tradition and with insight into the sociopolitical context in which it finds itself. It must become clear whom it will serve and how it can best forward the realization of the kingdom. It cannot avoid having a political dimension and impact. Thus, it must become conscious and intentional about the political impact for which it strives. Within Latin America, the only credible political option is one that gives preferential care to the poor.

Within conditions of poverty and powerlessness, and given the influence the church does have in Latin America, it must create conditions for its people to become aware and active in questions of social justice. It must help them see the religious dimension of political activity and the political dimension of religious activity. The church must awaken their sense of justice and internally organize itself as a community of and for justice, enhancing mutuality among its members, providing them with a space for action and creative speech, and instilling sensitivity to the needs of the poor. It should make people shake away their conformity to the present state of affairs. In Gutiérrez's words:

> If a situation of injustice and exploitation is incompatible with the coming of the Kingdom, the Word that announces this coming ought normally to point out this incompatibility. This means that the people who hear this message and live in these conditions by the mere fact of hearing it should perceive themselves as oppressed and feel impelled to seek their own liberation. Very concretely, they should "feel their hunger" and become aware that this hunger is due to a situation which the Gospel repudiates. The annunciation of the Gospel, thus, has a conscienticizing function, or in other words, a politicizing function.[73]

Although the community of faith discovers its true meaning within its commitment to the struggle of liberation, it cannot be strictly identified with those who are involved in this struggle nor with the community that struggles to liberate the poor. It is part of this historical struggle and of those who make it concrete, but it also has a character, identity, and mission of its own that cannot be reduced to the struggle to free the poor. To become oblivious to this distinction is the way toward violating the integrity of both the revolutionary struggle and the community of faith.

The church has the particular mission of explicitly proclaiming the Christ event and the implications of the saving grace of Christ. This is the memory the church must celebrate and strive to make concrete. To quote Míguez Bonino:

> The Church . . . is commissioned to proclaim God's salvation in Jesus Christ. This means, in traditional terms, the forgiveness of sins, namely, man's freedom in God's grace to take up again, in whatever circumstances and after whatever failure and destruction, the work committed to him in creation. It means, also in traditional terms, the call to the sanctification of man, namely, the invitation to effective love and the freedom to love. The Church is itself when it witnesses to God's saving activity in Jesus Christ, that is, when it makes clear God's renewed authorization, commandment, and liberation to man to be human, to create his own history and culture, to love and to transform the world, to claim and exercise the glorious freedom

of the children of God. The Church's distinct . . . claim is that the fullness of this humanity is given in the explicit, faithful, and grateful acknowledgment of Jesus Christ.

The Church, that is, the fellowship of those who embrace a historical task in the freedom of God's forgiveness and sanctification, cannot exist except as it concretely celebrates this freedom, reflects on it, and proclaims it. This is the meaning of the *disciplina arcana*, the specific and peculiar practices of the confessing community. . . . Such discipline has no meaning except insofar as it is related to, . . . the concrete creational praxis of these Christians. But such praxis has no Christian meaning . . . unless it is celebrated in the community of faith.[74]

The Latin American Church has consistently sided with the rich and powerful. It is in need, thus, of undergoing a process of repentance and of political and spiritual conversion. It must recognize and confess its practical and ideological negation of the forces of justice and assume a more intentional commitment to the process by which the poor seek their liberation. This would be a conversion from injustice to justice, from the celebration of death to the proclamation of life in abundance for the poor and marginal.

It must take steps to free itself from those who, being the "owners of the goods of the world," have always attempted to remain "owners of the Gospel," and used it to justify their self-interest and position of authority. If the church can free itself from the hold of the present power structure, then it can make practical and concrete what it proclaims theoretically, that within its walls there is true freedom for its members to choose among the alternative political options available to them. Hugo Assmann, being less optimistic about the possibility of a revolutionary church, demands that the church at least fulfill its promises of allowing people to make a free political option. The idea of a church that serves as the ideological justification of the status quo, even a revolutionary status quo, is rejected by all liberation theologians.

Revolutionary Christians must know that their revolutionary task, although it implies their effective participation in the conquest of power by the exploited, does not end there. Their revolution is a permanent task that does not allow itself to be completed in this world. It is not a matter of taking advantage of the occasion and then accommodating oneself to the new situation. However, this revolutionary perspective cannot dispense with the need to take sides and be concretely involved in the struggle.[75]

A church that seeks to serve the poor must itself become poor. It must live a life that is not offensive to the state of misery and deprivation the poor are forced to live in. What is more important, it must be a church that shares concretely in their values and aspirations. This is not to romanticize and make the dehumanization and denigration that poverty necessarily entails a virtue. Rather, it calls the church to become a part of that struggle that seeks to overcome this condition that is an offense to humanity, an offense to God, and a detriment to the realization of God's kingdom. As Gutiérrez explains,

> Poverty—the results of social injustice, which has its deepest roots in sin—is accepted, not in order to make it an ideal of life, but in order to witness to the evil it represents. The condition of the sinner, and its consequences, were accepted by Christ, not to idealize them, but out of love and solidarity with men, and to redeem them from sin; to fight against human egotism and abolish all injustice and division among men. . . . the witness of poverty lived as an authentic imitation of Christ, instead of separating us from the world, places us at the very heart of the situation of despoilment and oppression, and from there proclaims liberation and full communion with the Lord.[76]

The community of faith does have a number of contributions to make to the struggle for liberation. This struggle calls for an identification with and understanding of the lifestyle and worldview of the poor. Within Latin America, the Christian faith has influenced this lifestyle and worldview. The expectations, value system, and references of meaning of the poor have been very much influenced by the Christian faith. Thus, it is impossible in this region to be anti-Christian and revolutionary.

Liberation theologians argue that the distorted function Christianity has played in Latin America can be overcome. They claim that it is possible to rediscover the potential mobilizing and motivating power of the faith, as well as its historicizing, humanizing, and liberating criteria for revolutionary social change. Christians engaged in the struggle for liberation have a special duty to undertake this task of unblocking the present religious mentality which makes the poor fearful of committing themselves to the process of liberation and supports the situation of injustice. As Christians, they are more appreciative of the values and the relevance of their faith in enabling the poor to become beings of praxis capable of determining their own destiny. They are also more trustworthy and persuasive in bringing forth the true dynamic and humanizing dimension integral to a life of faith. Hugo Assmann declares:

> A theology that keeps pace with the revolutionary commit-
> ment of Christians and defines itself as critical reflection on
> their actions, has to concern itself with revolution: not to ele-
> vate itself to the rank of Professor of Revolution, but to assist
> in freeing the ideological brakes that keep some Christians tied,
> in the name of faith, to reactionary systems supporting the
> established order. . . . It must also make an effective contribu-
> tion to the permanent presence of a critical consciousness at
> the heart of the revolutionary process.[77]

Humanists can assume full responsibility for the task of creating the more just social order and the new person. This responsibility, however, can become a source of anxiety and fear that can make us betray the revolutionary and humanizing purpose. Confronted by the conflicts, contradictions, and un-certainties that define the political realm, and given our finite, partial, and limited understanding of the processes that take place within this realm, and our incapacity to control the final outcome of our actions, humanists are always tempted to seek immediate results, even when that involves the compromise of our ultimate goals. Our awareness of finitude makes the tempta-tion even greater. In the name of achieving some results, we tend to sacrifice the values and purposes we brought to the revolutionary process.

Members of the community of faith, on the other hand, have the advantage of being conscious that we have been freed from the task of achieving the promised kingdom of peace and justice by our own efforts. Thus, we can be free from this source of anxiety. We are aware that there is no historical power that can prevent the realization of the kingdom. As Míguez Bonino reminds us,

> beyond our toil and effort, our commitment and seriousness, our concern and responsibility, lies the certainty of God's own promise. We do not carry the burden of the whole world on our back, we carry only the burden of the day. We can rest![78]

Freed from the anxiety that comes from attempting to concretely fulfill the task of creating the kingdom of peace, justice, and the new person, Christians are freed for a more resolute and radical commitment to the realization of this historical project. We work under the assurance that whatever good we are capable of will be fulfilled to the fullest by the saving grace of God. Our mistakes and pitfalls will be forgiven and overcome by this same grace. Thus Christians ought to be willing to take risks, to make decisions, and to take a stand, even though we do not have total knowledge of circumstances and total assurance of the outcome of our actions.

Christians live under the promise of the resurrected Christ. We are assured not only that those actions that share in the quality of life of the promised kingdom have final reality at their side but also that we will share in Christ's everlasting life. This assurance, thus, enables us to be committed to the fullest, to accept the sacrifices which are intrinsic to the revolutionary project. We do not carry the burden of the whole world on our back.

Sacrifices are part of every struggle for social change. Still, it is unjust to concentrate the burdens of this process on a given sector. There is always an ethical dimension that must be taken into consideration. "Sacrifices can only be requested with a consideration of the human and ethical factors and, most importantly, when it is done justly: for all."[79] The injustices suffered now are never compensated later. One must have a long-range perspective and the vision of the penultimate character of the struggle for justice in spite of one's radical commitment to it. This will give endurance and patience in upholding the moral element within the struggle. As Míguez Bonino says,

> there can be no "teleological suspension of ethics," . . . no human class, group or generation can be considered as merely instrumental. . . . such calculations of human cost and suffering cannot be separated from human, ethical considerations. It cannot be merely a question of tactics. And this for two reasons: One is that no human group or class can be made the exclusive and definitive bearer of evil in history. . . . [and] it cannot erase the power of the risen Christ present in all humanity. . . . Wherever there is a human face there is evil and hope, and therefore ethical considerations must be upheld. Secondly, . . . a revolutionary process is not for the Christian the "final sprint" in which humanity can exhaust the last human and moral breath, but only a stage . . . in a long continuously conflictive pilgrimage. Every generation, . . . is at the same time means and end, the bearer of sacrifice and the inheritor of hope, called to realize as fully as possible all the human possibilities open to it (politically, socially, economically, spiritually) and called to suffer and to toil for new and greater possibilities for future generations. No really human achievement can be obtained through the denial of the humanity of some men or of a generation.[80]

# 3

## LIBERATION JUSTICE
## AND ALTERNATIVE CONCEPTS
## OF JUSTICE
## IN THE WESTERN WORLD
●

Liberation theologians present their concept of justice as an alternative to other concepts of justice that are influential within Latin America and the Western world. It is seen as an alternative to the natural law concept of justice that predominates in Roman Catholic thought, the positive law conception of justice that predominates in legal practice today, and the natural right conception of justice central to liberal capitalist thought. The intention of this chapter is to clarify some dimensions of the liberation concept of justice by comparing it to these alternatives. Since we proceed by using ideal types, it must be clear that no ideal type can in fact exhaust the richness of meaning of each of the alternatives presented nor the plurality of possibilities with their particular nuances.

### The Natural Law Concept of Justice[1]

Traditional Roman Catholic thought argues that questions of justice are best understood within the framework of natural law. In this perspective reality consists in a well-ordered objective structure created by God's eternal law, the embodiment of God's reason. Natural law is nothing but the rational creature's participation in the eternal law that is at the basis of all creation.

Although the determination of the just is a rational enterprise, it cannot be determined by autonomous reason. It must be determined by reason informed by eternal law, that is, by theonomous reason. Human reason can partake of eternal law. It is from this objective structure that it must derive the values to organize individual, social, and political life. Our self-realization and the well-being of the community depend on our capacity to discern, imitate, and adapt to this ontological system of law. It provides us with objective criteria of justice to regulate our mutual dealings (particular justice) and our dealings with society as a whole (general justice). Questions of law and justice are never merely conventional. It is essential and morally obligatory that we give ourselves laws that are derived from or correspond to natural law. It is our unique dignity that God has inclined and empowered us to be able to do so.

An intrinsic unity exists between the realm of fact and the realm of value. All dimensions of human existence have a moral dimension. Justice, the correct ordering of human relationships in terms of what is due to each, is a moral virtue. It is the virtue concerned with the good of the other and the common good. As a virtue, justice concerns itself not only with what we do but also with whom we become in the process of acting in a certain way and pursuing certain ends. Justice seeks to create in us the perpetual disposition of giving to others what is due to them, as determined by the natural order of things.

Natural law thinking establishes what is just, lawful, and right in two ways: either through deduction from the objective natural order accessible to all rational beings from which we can arrive at the principles of moral life or through induction from the way human beings act and have acted in the past, observing the actions and inclinations they unveil. In both cases we are able to discern what our true ends are.

In the first case, the ultimate structure of reality is perceived as static and determinative of the substance of justice. In the second case, the structure of value is seen as more dynamic. More attention is given to historical and social circumstances and to subjective feelings of the actors. There is a greater disposition to rethink what justice entails in changing circumstances. In both cases it is assumed that there is a human essence beneath all appearances and accidents that can be unveiled by reason, an essence that is the foundation for our concept of justice. There is a realm of truth which is complete in itself, from which we can know how things ought to be. The life of praxis is an application of what theoretically can be perceived as certain, true, and desirable.

Natural law and natural justice are normative for positive laws. The value of laws is not founded upon their capacity to preserve order and peace but mainly upon their being in accord with natural law. Positive laws based on a source other than natural law do not have the same obligatory and imperative character as true law. Laws are obligatory not just because they are enacted by legitimate authority but because of their correspondence to the natural order of things. Laws that violate the precepts of natural law are only a semblance of law. In fact, they are an act of violence. We abide by them not out of respect but either out of fear of the punishment that results from disobeying them or the advantages we can derive from complying with them. Natural law thinkers argue that the more particular the problems laws are enacted to deal with, the farther they are from being derived directly from natural law. Such laws build more on the wisdom of the community and human convention. Still they are valid insofar as they are consistent with natural law. Only good laws can appeal to our moral conscience and enable us to persuade others of their intrinsic worth.

It is clear for natural law theorists that not even the best system of laws can be simply identified with natural law. Even the best system of laws cannot avoid making use of the social instruments of violence to enforce it and assure people of their rights. Within every social order, there are those who refuse to abide by the laws and disregard the rights of others. They must be coerced to obey and act in conformity with the law.

In the natural law tradition morality and legality are intimately related. Still they are not identified with nor reduced to each other. Positive laws are concerned with the social dimension of our existence and with the external conformity of our actions to what is prescribed by the laws. Moral laws are primordially concerned with our individual existence and concern themselves not just with external behavior but also with the subjective motives of our actions. Morality has to be freely accepted. It cannot be coerced. Moral actions result from our conviction of the correctness of the action rather than from fear of any type of social coercion. To recognize the difference between morality and legality does not deny the underlying fact that they are inevitably interwoven and determine each other.

The claim that positive laws are subject to the criteria of natural justice is not intended to diminish the value and importance of positive laws. Positive laws make social life possible; they enable us to enjoy a stable social existence. They also make us aware of what our rights are and what we can expect from others and from society as a whole. Positive laws cannot be disregarded casually. Compliance with the prevailing system of law is as strong in the natural law tradition as it is in the positive law conception of justice.

The claim that we can determine our natural inclinations and true ends by observing past human behavior and that we must adapt to the objective, normative structure that underlies reality has made the natural law theory somewhat conservative. It has tended to identify the status quo with what ought to exist by nature. It also tends to preserve traditional customs and practices. Historically speaking the natural law concept of justice has never sought to provide a justification for social change or the transformation of the status quo. Its intention has always been to preserve a social order and stability which is seen as conducive to peace and justice. Appeals to natural justice were usually raised to remind those in power of their obligation to fulfill their duties toward the less advantaged as dictated by custom.

Feudal society is an example of a society organized under the ideology of natural law. Its hierarchical ordering was seen as a reflection of the hierarchical order of the cosmos. It was a static and tradition-oriented society. Each social stratum had clearly defined social functions. A person's social position and function were determined at birth, as were the rights and duties related to them. Religiously speaking, there was a recognition of the basic equality of all human beings. Equality, however, was limited to the religious realm. Socially and politically speaking, equality was nonexistent and perceived as detrimental to the very possibility of social existence. Justice called for the equal treatment of equals. This equality was interpreted as proportional equality—members of the same social stratum were to be treated equally—but there was to be no equality between members of different social strata. According to this notion of proportional equality, it was just that the few controlled the wealth and power and the many were dependent upon them.

The conservative character of natural law thinking is also revealed in the function of positive laws within society. Positive laws by and large merely consolidated the expectations that had become customary within society. They gave legal sanction to the traditional way of doing things. When natural law and justice were cited to challenge the law, it was merely to challenge a practice that violated the traditional way of doing things.

Rights granted privileges as well as obligations or duties to those who bore them. Among the duties and responsibilities of the powerful was attending to and caring for the needs of the poor who were dependent on them. Personal ties existed among the members of society that made it impossible for the powerful to disregard the need claims of the poor.[2] Need, however, was not recognized as a valid criterion of justice. The needs of the poor were to be attended to on the basis of charity or prudence, not as a matter of justice. It was another way of preserving social stability, of acting according to social expectations.

While natural law theory tends to be conservative, it is not incapable of adapting to different historical circumstances. It has proven its capacity to be relevant for a social context quite different from feudalism. The theological and sociopolitical work of Jacques Maritain is a good example of the adaptive capabilities of natural law thinking. In his work, natural law expresses and advocates the values of liberal capitalism, a social order which could be interpreted as radically negating feudalistic values.

Maritain was instrumental in enabling the Roman Catholic Church to come to terms with and accept the values of liberal capitalism. His sociopolitical views have enabled and inspired a significant sector of the Roman Catholic Church to renew its concern and commitment to issues of social justice. This has been particularly true in Latin America. Maritain was one of the great theological figures who argued for the autonomy of the world and the political commitments of the members of the community of faith. He argued that the church cannot be paternalistic regarding the political options of Christians and that it should surrender its tutelage over the worldly activities of its members. Within the context of a Christendom mentality, this claim of freedom was quite radical.

In agreement with the natural law tradition, Maritain sustains the view that persons as persons are the bearers of rights which others, society, and the state cannot disregard. These rights, more than anything else, place others under the obligation not to intervene with the exercise of our freedom. In agreement with modern liberalism these rights call us not to adapt to a given state of affairs but to initiate new processes and to be creative in all aspects of life. Persons are to be consulted in all matters that affect their lives in a fundamental way. They are entitled to express their consent in such matters.

Maritain recognizes that rights do change historically, both in terms of the nature of the rights and in terms of who has them. There is also a recognition of the phenomenon of social mobility and thus of the fact that persons change both their social function and the rights and obligations entailed in these functions. What one does and what one achieves are determinative for what one is justly entitled to; tradition cannot establish this on a permanent basis.

Although Maritain's position is much more progressive than that presented in classical natural law thinking, one still can detect a conservative bent. One sees him contributing to the consolidation of the status quo—in this case liberal capitalism—which has already proven itself an irreversible sociological fact. His critique of liberal capitalism tends to be moralistic, directed at the spirit of the system not at its structural foundation. He never questions the way the system goes about accumulating capital but rather questions its excesses, which he sees as capable of being solved if action is oriented by the proper principles. This emphasis on the spiritual dimension becomes clear when he rejects socialism, not on the basis of its capacity to distribute and accumulate wealth, but on its proclamation of religious beliefs.[3] It is ultimately the spiritual-moral dimension of society that must be changed for the system to work smoothly.

### Critique to the Natural Law Concept of Justice

Liberation theologians and natural law theorists agree at several points. Both assert that the Christian faith has something unique to contribute to our understanding of social justice. Both refuse the idea that "might makes right" and thus claim that justice is a criterion for positive laws. Both understand human nature in a social manner, as opposed to individualism, recognizing that the community has rights that place individuals under obligation. Finally, they both agree that having a right always implies having duties as well. It is regarding the particular content of these formal agreements that they disagree.

Liberation theologians are more biblically centered than natural law centered. The biblical stories for them emphasize more a historico-political God than a God creating a hierarchically ordered cosmos. Within Scripture itself they give special attention to the Exodus event (God the liberator), the resurrection narrative (God the giver, sustainer, and redeemer of life) and the prophetic tradition (God who takes sides with the poor and establishes justice for them). God is perceived as being present and active within history, creating conditions for the realization of new possibilities for the betterment of humanity.

Liberation theologians do not argue from a substantive notion of human nature in determining what rights people are entitled to. They have no fixed understanding of what human nature is, no sense of a human essence that can be known once and for all. Rights are justified as they enable persons to become historical actors—justified in terms of being necessary conditions for a person to become a being of praxis (a responsible sociohistorical actor). No human essence exists that can be known a priori and once and for all, an essence which is unfolding itself within history. Rather, only historically and socially conditioned interpretations of human nature exists, and they are very much the product of the way persons have organized their productive and political life. Thus, rights do not call us to adapt to an objective order but enable us to initiate new processes and to infuse history with purpose. They enable us to initiate new possibilities of life even beyond the status quo, an initiation that is not just functional but also creative of new social configurations.

Justice is a criterion of law, but the content of justice from a liberation perspective is not simply that we accept and adapt to the status quo nor is it limited to what has been traditionally accepted. Social justice has basic human needs as its material content. Its aim is the creation of an egalitarian society in which the worse off are able to enjoy the same opportunity to realize the level of well-being they are capable of as any other group in society. Human need is neither a matter of charity nor is it to be left to the will of individuals within society. The satisfaction of needs is a matter of justice and the responsibility of society as a whole, through the medium of the state. All members of society are called to contribute to the existence of a social institution whose business is the satisfaction of the needs of the poor with the purpose of empowering them to become responsible sociohistoric actors. The poor and powerless have a justice claim over those who have resources they need to become beings of praxis. Justice is not the product of social stability and order. Rather, at times, it demands the transformation of those social conditions that make it impossible for the worse off within society to improve their condition. Peace is more than the absence of conflict. It is the creation of conditions that enable all members of society to obtain fullness of life.

Liberation theologians are thus very critical of the conservative bent of natural law thinking regarding justice. In their view, this theoretical framework, in Míguez Bonino's words, "sacralizes a static and stratified society," making direct and careless identifications between the natural order of things and the existing ones. Lack of awareness of historical conditioning left this ethic unprotected against the temptation of passing off as divine or natural what was only the expression of interest or the balance of power.[4]

Liberation theologians are also critical of the relationship natural law theory establishes between theory and practice. In spite of their quest for ultimate synthesis, a gap persists between the realm of metaphysical truths and theological certainties and the historical actions men and women are engaged in. According to the natural law tradition, truth is distinct and independent of its historical efficacy. It exists in itself, is eternal, and can be grasped by pure reason. The most conservative interpretation of truth also makes the politically conservative argument that only the church hierarchy is able to correctly interpret and deduce from the natural order of things what we must do. More modern and progressive versions of natural law theory have appealed to an inductive method of arriving at what is dictated by the natural order. This has made them more sensitive to historical thinking and to prevailing social conditions in the process of determining what people ought to do. Still, the relationship between theory and practice and the determination of truthfulness is not understood in dialectical terms.

Thus, in natural law theory, praxis has been reduced to application of what is held to be theoretically correct. It is not itself an integral part of determining what is truth. Nor does practice question in any fundamental way what is held as true. Truth is a matter of correspondence with what has been established as the essence of being. It is not a matter of sociohistorical transformation and recreation. Justice and rights can be determined and defined prior to, and independently of, our historical participation in bringing them about. Such participation can at best only confirm what has already been established by reason. The ideal guides the concrete practice of women and men rather than allowing the concrete ways people have organized themselves to determine their interpretation of what is valuable. For liberation theologians this constitutes a negation of what is basic to a correct understanding of justice, as well as what is necessary to strengthen the consciousness and organization of the poor in their struggle to bring about justice. Justice can only be properly defined in the activity of bringing it about in light of the concrete situations that limit its realization. This is what gives justice its dynamic, forward-looking quality. Modes of thought that separate theory from praxis, be those modes distinctions of plane theories or two-kingdom theories, tend to be both idealistic and conservative.[5] It is praxis, the efficient transformation of our social world, that will ultimately confirm and reveal the possibilities, as well as the limitations, of our particular understanding of justice.

Within Latin America, natural law thinkers have consistently opted for conservative political stances. At best, they have provided ideological support to third-way "alternatives" which at moments of social crisis have opted consistently for the status quo. Christian Democratic parties within Latin America provide a good example of this.[6] These political parties, which intend to respond to the social doctrines of the Catholic Church, have sought to create an alternative political option to forward the cause of social justice. Jacques Maritain was the ideological mentor of these political movements, along with figures like Roger Vekemans, one of its most articulate defenders within Latin America. Both authors have been defenders of modern freedoms and have sought to separate the autonomy of the political decisions of lay Catholics from the paternalistic influence of the church. They contributed much to the awakening of Christians to concern for the issues of social justice and to active involvement in improving the condition of those worse off within society.

For liberation theologians, the weakness of these political

parties is their incapacity to recognize that the realization of their goals necessitates a radical transformation of the social structure. They are not able to come to terms with the need to move beyond social reform and to initiate a new process of social transformation which presents an alternative historical project to the one of liberal capitalism.

At the theoretical level Christian Democratic parties presented a third way between capitalism and socialism, the unique Christian alternative that represents a synthesis between the best of capitalism and the best of socialism. Put forward as a new historical project that preserves the freedom of the individual while preserving at the same time a strong sense of communal responsibility, it proposed to overcome both the dangers of totalitarianism and egoistic individualism which are intrinsic to both social systems. Their slogan "Revolution in Freedom" captures the ideological substance of their position.

However, the independent and unique alternative that was given theoretical expression did not materialize at the level of concrete political options. While theoretically they presented a critical and viable option between capitalism and socialism, practically, they have always opted for capitalism against socialism. They have even found themselves betraying policies that they presented as integral to their identity. Confronted with the misery and growing militancy of the poor, they have opted to limit their social policies to those of crisis containment rather than programs of basic social change, reform rather than revolution, freedom rather than equality.

### The Positive Law Concept of Justice[7]

The positive law concept of justice upholds that it is best to deal with questions of law apart from questions of morality and justice. The question of whether or not there is an objective norm for positive laws is beyond the competence of the jurist. As far as the construction of an adequate system of law to regulate the mutual dealings of citizens is concerned, such issues are at best of doubtful value.

Justice is best understood within the limits of legality or of positive law itself. What is just and right is determined by the prevailing system of law. A just person is one who acts in agreement with what the law dictates. The validity of law is very much dependent on command and obedience. It must be enacted by legitimate authority. This, in itself, makes it just; it must be obeyed because it is law. It is irrelevant to bring forth questions of morality and religion when one wants to understand what laws are and what they entail.[8]

As many valid concepts of justice exist as there are legitimate systems of law and constitutional systems. There are no objective and universally valid criteria to judge between the various alternatives. Notions of human nature, claims of divine revelation, and other groundings or expressions of moral evaluation merely express an arbitrary and subjective preference of value by the one who posits them. The obligation implied by the law does not depend on our coming to agree with its moral content. It is based solely on the fact that it is law. Morality provides no excuse regarding our obligation to comply with the law.

There are times in which it is necessary to change a particular law. This concept of justice has no problem if one law is changed. What is unacceptable is the view that the system of law be changed. There are too many risks involved in such actions and little or no benefit to be expected. One of the reasons to keep considerations of morality separate from those of legality is precisely to prevent revolutionary idealists from violating the laws in the name of some higher law, or some normative concept of justice, and to prevent those in power from sacralizing the status quo and opposing necessary changes in particular laws.

Even those who uphold the positivist concept of justice recognize that every system of law embodies within it a moral option. They recognize that the prevailing system of law conditions one's moral options but argue that it does not determine the whole of morality. Laws and values cannot but determine each other. Every attempt to reform and enact laws is always an attempt to reform and enact values. Whatever moral system is present within the system of law, however, is as arbitrary and as subjective as any other alternative.

## Critique to the Positive Law Concept of Justice

Liberation theologians denounce as unjust the system of law that legitimizes the structure of dependence. For them, positive laws are not ultimate, no matter who enacts them. Positive laws are not to be taken lightly. They do create conditions for peace and human creativity. Without the regularity and stability created by positive laws, social existence would not be possible. They also enable us to have a clear sense of our rights and what they entitle us to, the basis for raising justice claims. Yet, these elements of positive law are not enough for liberation theologians. The moral content of the law is still a relevant criterion in determining the validity of the law. As Miranda reminds us, "It is moral right, not physical power, that we are obliged to obey."[9] Coercion must remain a secondary or derivative quality of the law. It is precisely because laws are not defined primordially in terms of coercion that it is meaningful to speak of law and justice in a context broader than that of the nation state. It is meaningful, for example, to speak of law and justice in the international realm even though there is no coercive power nor apparatus to enforce laws. To abide by the system of law that sustains the structure of dependence might be legal but it will never be just, and not even the commands of a divine authority can make them just according to Miranda:

> No authority can decree that everything is permitted; for justice and exploitation are not so indistinguishable. And Christ died so that we might know that not everything is permitted.

> We are dealing with injustice, and there is no compensation for injustice. Any god who has not come to undo the hell that we have made of this life is a cruel god, even if there is another life. Even if the god of the theologians is not responsible for the barbarous world in which we live, the mere fact that he intervenes in our history for ends other than the abolition of human injustice qualifies him as amoral and merciless. . . . The omnipo-

tence of an amoral god could *compel me* to submission, but not *oblige* me to obedience. Not only should we refuse to worship and obey such a god, we should also be morally obliged to struggle against him, even if faced with certain defeat and condemnation to eternal torment. It is moral right, not physical power, that we are obliged to obey.[10]

Not to denounce and struggle against an unjust system of laws is a way of perpetuating and being an accessory to the injustice being committed.

When laws lose sight of their moral content, when they become things in themselves, they are likely to become instruments of oppression and injustice. It is important to free laws from being concerned merely with legislation and to keep them sensitive to the fact that we are dealing with persons that cannot always be treated in terms of cold impartiality and objectivization. Míguez Bonino writes:

> The legalistic person loses his capacity to relate himself with others in a dynamic and immediate way. He can only understand his relationships with God and others as the fulfillment of an impersonal contract and the duties and rights it allows. Relationships have become a tabulation of having fulfilled or not having fulfilled the contractual obligations that make God and neighbor objects. Shortly the person becomes dehumanized. . . .
>
> The law makes it impossible for [a person] to assume responsibility for his own moral life: he limits himself to following the rules, like the employee that punches the clock at the office, but who does not make any decision, which is the same as not being a man. He loses sight of the deepest and most humane intention of the law. Curiously enough he even reaches the point of negating this deepest and most human intention of the law in the process of abiding by it. . . .
>
> . . . The legalist pretends that in abiding by what the law demands he has reached a kind of good conduct that is self-justifying. He thus reserves for himself the center of his being and presents to God and his neighbor a list of duties achieved. In reality God and his neighbor are of interest to him as witnesses to his legal rectitude and as givers of the reward that that rectitude entails. The object of his actions is himself. . . . The law has become a tool at the service of a man enclosed upon himself and man finds himself satisfied with this situation. The

purpose of the law has been completely destroyed: it no longer leads to a mature moral life, nor does it open man to God and his neighbor, nor does it make him aware of his own sin. On the contrary, it has become the source in which man protects himself from God and others.[11]

From a liberation perspective, it is precisely the moral quality of law that gives it its dynamic character, making those concerned for justice seek what ought to be and push what exists to its limits. It is also what enables us to recognize the importance of laws without making them ultimate nor absolute. Within our religious tradition, the members of the community of faith cannot surrender their responsibility to evaluate laws in the light of what they perceive is the historical purpose of a God who has justice as a central concern. For Miranda,

> The injustice, the mercilessness, the oppression, and the exploitation to which all cultures have learned to resign themselves are precisely what Yahweh wants to abolish in the world. The great purpose of God's intervention in human history is definitively to eliminate all this injustice and enmity which many Christians, it would appear, find so normal.[12]

Regarding the issue of social justice, liberation theologians argue that the needs of the poor provide the most adequate criterion. Positive laws must create a social state of affairs that enables the poor to overcome their present condition of powerlessness and misery. If there is one issue all liberation theologians come together on, then it is their religious conviction that the core of divine revelation makes the needs of the poor the criterion of justice. It is also this criterion that frees contemporary pluralism from lacking any substance and remaining vague and open ended. As Miranda declares:

> The only meaning of law is to do justice, in the strictest, most social sense of the word. . . . And there is no doubt that it is the justice which saves the poor and the oppressed. . . .

> The protection of the weak is an imperative always in force, a responsibility which we cannot discharge by means of the letter of the law. And if the law constitutes a fixing and a bridling of the divine intervention which liberates the helpless, then this law militates against the will of God.[13]

## The Natural Right Concept of Justice[14]

Many authors, among them Maritain, claim that the natural right concept of justice which emerged and consolidated itself within liberal capitalism is intrinsically related to the natural law theory of justice. They both share a number of beliefs and convictions, among the most significant, the conviction that there are objective norms to which positive laws must conform. Ronald Dworkin, for example, argues that natural rights "are not the product of any legislation, or convention, or hypothetical contract," nor are they "simply the product of deliberate legislation or explicit social custom, but are independent grounds for judging legislation and custom."[15] In this perspective too, questions of legality are intrinsically related to questions of morality.

In spite of these and other similarities between these concepts of justice, it is important to point to that which makes them different. Both Maritain and d'Entrèves enable us to recognize the difference. They both make us aware that with Hugo Grotious a new development occurred within the natural law tradition. Maritain interpreted it as a distortion and deterioration of tradition, since it was a conception of natural law independent of religious substance. D'Entrèves sees it as a new beginning, a new and unique theory of law and justice.[16] Following d'Entrèves, we shall consider the three main characteristics which make natural right distinct from the natural law concept of law and justice: its rationalism, its individualism, and its radicalism.

The natural right concept of justice does not proclaim the existence of an objective structural order, be it static or dynamic, created by God from which to deduce human rights. Natural rights are grounded in the persons themselves, not on some objective cosmos or metaphysical order. They can be unveiled, understood, and argued for on the basis of reason alone. In matters of justice and rights, the realm of faith and religion has no foundational role or explanatory power. Autonomous reason is enough. It is important to remind ourselves that this concept of justice emerged as part of the struggle for liberation from religious domination. Questions of justice were no longer under the jurisdiction of experts who were presumed to have the insight to deduce from God's cosmos the true ends of humanity and the proper social and personal behavior for everyone to follow. Questions of justice and rights are the concern of all rational beings. Being rational is the only necessary requirement to be included in debates of this sort. Thus, these are issues to be dealt with within a public forum which is inclusive of the plurality of perspectives that are representative of the community in which all have an equal opportunity to express their views on these matters.

Natural rights are seen as moral properties which bestow upon each individual a unique dignity. To have a right is understood as having the freedom to self-initiate. Others are placed under the obligation of not intervening. There is no sense of conforming to a given objective structure. Rather, the emphasis is on initiating new activities, creating new institutions, and creating new social relationships. Persons have rights-interests to assert, not just functions to execute.

The natural right theory of justice allows for more than mere resistance to an unjust government, to the illegitimate use of power and authority, and to unjust laws. It recognizes the legitimacy of engaging in revolutionary social action. If a given social order and the system of law that sustains it violate our human rights, then it is both desirable and legitimate to transform it in a fundamental way. D'Entrèves argues that in the natural right tradition the concept of right becomes a "liberating principle, ready to hand for the use of modern man in his challenge to existing institutions."[17]

In the context of a feudal society, the natural right conception of justice is in fact a liberating principle. It challenges at its base the stability of the feudal order replacing it with a social order that seeks to remain open and dynamic. It creates a mental attitude that tends to undermine tradition and customs and emphasize instead the possibility and goodness of constantly creating new alternatives and ways of life. Growth, change, and forward looking attitudes are integral elements of this new ethos. Thus, it sustains a society that in principle rejects a fixed arrangement of social function and the rights they entail.

Society is understood in contractual terms. It is the product of a contract between individuals who are willing to enter a social agreement on the condition that they would derive from society at least as much as they have contributed to it. From the outset, the concern for freedom and a sense of justice based on the criterion of distribution according to merit are built into the constitutional organization of society. These two concerns have remained central to classical and modern capitalism.

Classical capitalism understands society and the state as organizations whose sole purpose is to assure and maximize freedom for the individual. Society must establish procedures and the state must be limited so that individuals are able to exercise their freedom and pursue their life plans, i.e., interests, goals, activities, choices, decisions. The individual must remain the center and source of all authority. People must have a voice in the establishment and function of all institutions that in one way or another affect their existence in a fundamental way. Thus, a political mechanism of consent is essential to a just social order.

It is important that persons have the opportunity to achieve the level of well-being they are able to on the basis of the free use of their talents and resources. They must be free to use their talents and resources as they see fit to achieve their self-interest and meet the self-interest of others and of society as a whole. Distribution of social goods and services ought to take place on the basis of some criterion of desert, be it effort, contribution, merit, or similar criteria. A free and competitive market mechanism provides the best method of assuring that distribution will correspond to individual desert and merit. As long as the market is kept competitive, free, clear of political interference, social laws are obeyed, and contracts freely engaged in and faithfully abided by, the final outcome and distribution will be just. Justice in this perspective is not determined by a specific goal. There is no way of determining that a specific distributive outcome is just. Only procedures can be evaluated as just. End results are just only as the outcome of a just procedure.

It is clear that the procedures of the marketplace will result in the unequal distribution of social goods and burdens. But there is no violation of justice if these inequalities reflect the inequalities of talent, skills, effort, and contribution of those who were participating and competing in the marketplace. People should enjoy the benefits of the rewards of their labor as well as take responsibility for their failures. Justice, insofar as rights are concerned, seeks the preservation and maximization of freedom. It has no concern with social equality. In fact social equality is seen as detrimental to an efficient productive process since it deprives people of necessary incentives to produce. The possibility of enjoying greater wealth and power is an important incentive for people to produce to the best of their abilities. Efficient production is expected to benefit not just those who produce, but society as a whole.

Social equality is not a desirable goal; it not only threatens to take away the incentive to produce but also is too costly, as the general well-being of all members of society suffers. It also represents a violation of the right to freedom and a denial of the inevitable inequality which is the natural outcome of our mutual dealings. It can only be achieved through the installment of a totalitarian state. The only legitimate equality the state must concern itself with is political equality. All persons must be equally protected in the exercise of political and personal self-determination. Socioeconomic equality is viewed as an illegitimate intervention in the right to self-determination.

The natural right concept of justice, like the natural law concept of justice, argues that the poor do not have, as a matter of justice, the right to have their needs met. Natural law justice recognized that the powerful had the duty to attend to the needs of the poor who lived under their jurisdiction, if not as a matter of justice, at least as a matter of social charity and custom. However, even in this context, if acts of charity undermined social stability, the rich and powerful were free from this responsibility. The claim of need was secondary to the need to preserve social order. Natural right thinkers, in particular the most conservative ones, agree that need is not a legitimate criterion of justice. They see no causal connection between the concentration of wealth and power and the misery and powerlessness of the poor. Policies of social distribution have no moral foundation and thus are illegitimate as well as harmful. Those who feel that a more equitable distribution should exist have the means of using voluntary association to achieve their goals. The needs of the poor should be attended by the use of charity and the state cannot be called upon to use its powers to this end. People who do not want to contribute their resources voluntarily should not be coerced to do so.

Liberal capitalism has undergone significant changes. Its complacent attitude toward extreme socioeconomic and political inequality, its instrumental understanding of society, and its atomistic and radically individualistic concept of human nature have changed. Pure laissez-faire capitalism gave way to welfare state capitalism, and with it came a new concern to contain the gap between the rich and the poor, a renewed sense of the common good, and of the social nature of human beings.

The welfare state was part of the struggle of workers and other producers to make the state, and through it society as a whole, responsive to the needs of the worse off. The welfare state represents a new stage in the consciousness of a society which sees the need to use the state to correct and secure not only violations of our civil and political rights, but also extreme forms of socioeconomic inequality and thus preserve our socioeconomic rights.

A new consciousness emerged that proclaimed at one and the same time the preservation of the institution of private property and the free market, and the installation of a social institution whose business is to attend the needs of the poor. This has become so predominant that even the class of entrepreneurs justifies and rationalizes its commercial activities on the grounds of this new ideology. Now big business argues that its activities are not just to make profits but that its profits are justified only because they attend individual and social needs. The state is no longer seen as a necessary social evil but as a partner in improving the general well-being of society as a whole.

Society is no longer seen as a sum of individuals but as a structure of relationships whose preservation demands our contribution and which is an integral part of what it means to have a good life. A renewed sense of serving society has become predominant. David Miller suggests:

> The organized view of society . . . reintroduces the principle of need into the sphere of social justice, after it had been excluded by individualism. . . . organized society makes service to the community the dominant motive in work; the justification for rewarding the incumbent of one position more highly than the incumbent of another is that he makes a greater contribution to social well-being. But social well-being must eventually be broken down into individual benefits, and the chief constituent of individual well-being is the satisfaction of needs. Thus, the better-off can show their own rewards to be just by meeting the just claims to their services made by those in need. It is important here that the needy have a claim of *justice* to the benefits created by others, otherwise the notion of "service" degenerates into paternalistic charity.[18]

## Critique to the Natural Right Concept of Justice

Liberation theologians see justice as dynamic and ever-changing. For them, however, there is no necessity of limiting this dynamic to the logic of capitalism. If our rights and concepts of justice are to change in agreement with the ways we transform our social world, why then should we limit our struggle for justice to what is possible within capitalism? Liberal capitalism seems to have stopped the historical process and sees itself as the best socioeconomic order humanity is capable of. From its own internal perspective, it seems to claim that nothing new is possible, thus, that the quest for justice consists in a never-ending reform of the status quo.

Liberation theologians recognize that liberal capitalism represented a definite step forward in the realization of human rights and justice. It created objective and subjective conditions that allowed men and women to emancipate themselves from the stagnant hierarchical structures and fixed system of authority of feudal society. New possibilities to forward freedom and well-being were opened, as was the promise that all persons would become artisans of a new destiny.

Like all historical projects, liberal capitalism proved itself to be an ambiguous and contradictory historical process. While it promised everyone that they would be able to forward their freedom and well-being, as a matter of fact, it allowed only the few to attain these goals and to do so at the expense of the many. For poor nations and poor social classes, the capitalist ethos has become an ideological justification of a situation of domination:

> The movement for modern freedoms, democracy, and the universal and rational thought in Europe and the United States, meant for Latin America a new type of oppression and more cruel forms of despoilment of the poor classes. The exploitation carried out by the modern countries, champions of freedom, constituted a traumatic experience which cannot be forgotten when one speaks of freedom and democracy in the continent.[19]

Capitalism has generated inequalities of wealth and power among the members of society and between nations that it is unable to overcome. Liberation theologians argue that only a socialist society will give poor nations and social classes an opportunity to forward their freedom and well-being.

In rejecting capitalism, liberation theologians also reject the notions of justice and right that are intrinsic to it. Regarding the criterion of merit or desert, liberation theologians see it as an adequate criterion of justice in the sphere of law, but not in the sphere of social justice. Within the legal system the criterion of merit is very adequate. In the court of law, punishment must be given to those who have committed a crime without regard to consideration of need. Those who have violated a law deserve to be punished; those who have not ought not be punished. The same is true in the realm of prizes. Only those who have done something to deserve a prize should receive it. Even within private and public institutions, it seems just that offices and promotions within the ranks be given on the basis of the performance of the candidates.

Within the realm of social justice, the criterion of merit is not adequate and can in fact be very unjust. It is the criterion that has allowed the emergence of socioeconomic inequality and, thus, has created conditions to enable the few to exploit and dominate the many. It helps support an ideology of indifference toward the poor and powerless: they have what they deserve! What is more significant, the criterion of merit seems to negate the view that persons as persons are of equal worth and dignity. It sustains this view at the political level but disregards it at the socioeconomic level. For liberation theologians, the satisfaction of the needs that sustain life is beyond the category of merit. No one deserves to live under subhuman conditions or to have his or her dignity violated. A person must satisfy certain needs regardless of ability and effort, simply because one is part of the human family or because one thinks theologically and is aware she or he was created by God.

The principle of desert seems to be contradictory in another respect. It enables those who have been fortunate in the natural lottery and who have benefited from social and historical circumstances to appropriate for themselves what they have received through inheritance, for which they cannot be given any real credit. It seems contradictory to claim that a person is entitled to what she or he has worked for and at the same time allow persons to appropriate resources that are the result of natural endowment or historical accident. It also allows people to receive benefits or suffer penalties for things they are not responsible for, such as having or lacking a natural talent or being born at the right time and at the right place.

It also seems extremely difficult to determine within the context of a complex and collectivist productive process who is more deserving than others in the production of commonly produced goods and services. In this context, it is very difficult to determine what shares belong to each of the contributing parties. The criterion of desert also seems to encourage antisocial behavior and attitudes. The quest for greater economic reward encourages personal selfishness. One decides on what activities to engage oneself in not on the basis of their contribution to society but on the basis of personal gain. Also the interest of the individual takes precedence over the interest of society, leading to an egoistic understanding of human rights. Given the uncertainty of the market mechanism and the existence of an army of unemployed, the principle of desert undermines the possibility of social cooperation. Others are seen as a threat to our well-being rather than as potential partners for our mutual liberation.

Since the criterion of desert does not allow the poor to make claims of justice for the satisfaction of their needs, they are left to some form of public or private charity. This is humiliating for those who receive it, because it makes them aware of their dependence. It also creates in those who give it an attitude of condescension, because they make the poor act in ways that please them. In any case, both mutual respect and self-respect are lost. The practice of charity is an intrinsic part of Christian life. Christians understand that they are called to go the extra mile to give beyond what is required by law in order to alleviate the needs of the poor. Charity, however, is to be done in ways that will help the poor overcome their passivity and dependence and free the givers from the dangers of paternalistic arrogance that go hand in hand with their power of being able to give.

Liberation theologians argue that the criterion of need is able to overcome some of the distortions of the principle of desert. It makes it legitimate for the poor to claim as a matter of justice that their needs be attended. It creates social conditions in which the poor can confront other members of society as equals who have the obligation to assist them and enable them to become beings of praxis. This is an obligation that falls upon all members of society equally and whose final end is to empower the worse off to be able to assume their social responsibility. Equality and mutuality alone can free charity from the possible distortions of creating passive dependence in some and arrogance in others. Charity must always be placed in the context of justice. Only a social order that assures each of its members a share of what is socially produced can create a community aware that the rights it enjoys place it under the obligation to preserve a social order that cares for the well-being of the weakest members of society. As Miranda says:

> The fact that differentiating wealth is unacquirable without violence and spoliation is presupposed by the Bible in its pointed anathemas against the rich; therefore almsgiving is nothing more than restitution of what has been stolen, and thus the Bible calls it justice. . . . It all has to do with giving food to the hungry, drink to the thirsty, a home to the stranger, clothing the naked, etc.
>
> These are all works which the West calls charity, in contradistinction to justice. A frequent methodological error is to believe that the discrepancy is verbal or explicable by the alleged imperfection of biblical morality, which did not know how to distinguish between justice and charity. The discrepancy is a solid, unequivocal fact. To brand the biblical authors as primitive is a value judgement, not objective exegetical work. What is in question is precisely Western morality's alleged superiority to biblical morality.
>
> . . . when the Bible calls "justice" what Western culture calls "almsgiving" it is because the private ownership which differentiates the rich from the poor is considered unacquirable without violence and spoliation; the Fathers of the Church also understood this very clearly. The causal dependence which exists between the distribution of ownership and the distribution of income had led us, by economics alone, to the same conclusion. But it would be erroneous to think that this economic fact escaped the biblical authors.[20]

Classical natural right theory concerns itself exclusively with the right to freedom and sees all attempts to promote the value of equality as a violation of the right to freedom. The values of freedom and equality are interpreted as antagonistic to each other, for the latter always entails a loss of the former. Furthermore, equality is seen as harmful to social utility. This notion of justice is more concerned with the efficient allocation of resources for the sake of increasing social utility than with the issue of distribution. By increasing production, all members of society are likely to gain either directly or indirectly. From a liberation perspective, although the need to increase production is a major consideration of justice, it is not the only consideration. One must recognize that utility and justice considerations do at times conflict and that the latter should take precedence over the former. The principle of utility seeks the maximization of social production and is somewhat unconcerned with questions of distribution. The criterion of justice is a distributive criterion that seeks the creation and preservation of social equality. Utilitarianism has a tendency to equalize all interests and reduce them to the criterion of utility. In so doing it tends to add and subtract utility values, disregarding the uniqueness of the people whose utility is being pursued. It assumes that if a given state of affairs leads to the increase of average utility it is good and just. It does not recognize that the frustration of the interest of some is not compensated by the satisfaction received by the many. Justice makes us aware that all persons count as one and that the violation of their rights is not compensated by the satisfaction of the claims of the majority. Justice at times can demand that social utility be reduced. This is a political decision that must be made by the community and cannot just be taken for granted.

For liberation theologians the rights to freedom and well-being have an equal standing. As a matter of principle neither has priority over the other. Even though they do stress and seem to give priority to the right to well-being or to the pursuit of socioeconomic equality, it is not a matter of principle but one of political prudence and historical necessity. What is central for their notion of rights is that these two rights are intrinsically related, so that the realization of one necessitates the realization of the other. There are tensions between them; at times they do conflict and one has to make decisions as to which one must be given priority, but they are not in principle antagonistic. Thus, persons ought not only be assured the right for self-initiation but must also be empowered, that is, be provided the necessary resources and services to be able to self-initiate.

More contemporary formulations of capitalism have recognized this and have rejected the notion that there is an intrinsic antagonism between the right to freedom and the right to equality. This version, which is the one contemporary natural law thinkers also identify themselves with, upholds the priority of the right to freedom but understands that it is still possible to work for greater economic equality, at least to prevent the gap from getting larger, without in so doing undermining the right to freedom. In this view, the right to freedom not only calls for our nonintervention but at times it also calls on us to provide positive assistance. In this view, too, the quest for some reasonable level of equality is a legitimate concern of justice as is the protection and maximization of freedom.

Theoretically, welfare capitalism achieves the reconciliation between freedom and equality by establishing a clear and mutually exclusive distinction between the realm of politics proper and the socioeconomic realm. Questions of freedom belong to the former and questions of equality to the latter. Given this distinction between these spheres of human activity it is possible to work for equality without undermining freedom.

Liberation theologians argue that this dualism and the priority given to the right to freedom prevent arbitrariness and limit this concept of justice to seek short-term and pragmatic solutions to the problems confronted by the poor. This concept of justice cannot transcend its tendency simply to reform the status quo. If and when its supporters recognize that their goals cannot be achieved within the status quo, then they would rather abandon their goals than engage in the very difficult and long-term struggle of changing society. Liberation theologians do recognize that at times pragmatic and short-term solutions to enhance the well-being of the poor are the only thing possible. However, these short-term goals should not become an end in themselves but be made part of the organization and consciousness-raising activities of the larger revolutionary struggle.

Finally, liberation theologians question the procedural notion of justice that is intrinsic to liberal capitalism. Procedures are indeed important since they are intrinsic to our notion of fairness. Still by themselves they leave much to be desired.

Impartiality might be proper in a court of law, but when one is confronted with extreme misery and powerlessness, partiality for the poor is indispensable if justice is to be obtained. Democratic procedures are part of a just society, but in the absence of the class element which is part of true democracy, government by and for the poor or the majority, it loses its substance and true nature. Liberal capitalism is incapable of obtaining the liberation of the poor because for it the poor are not a primary concern but a secondary one to be dealt with mainly in moments of crisis and for the sake of maintaining social stability.

PART II

•

# JUSTICE
# AND
# ITS IMPLICATIONS
# FOR
# ECONOMICS AND
# POLITICS

•

# 4
# ECONOMIC JUSTICE

•

Questions of social justice are usually discussed within the economic realm. Justice is a distributive concept, concerned mainly with the question of how economic goods and social services are to be distributed among the members of society. The question of justice arises because the goods and services citizens need to be able to realize their individual and collective purposes are relatively scarce. Thus, as they proceed to press their claims on the available social goods and services, a conflictual situation is likely to emerge. This conflict makes it necessary to establish procedures and principles of distribution that seek mainly to regulate the basic structures of society, principles which citizens are able to recognize as fair and legitimate. The reality of relative scarcity makes it evident that justice is concerned not only with the distribution of economic and social benefits but also with the fair distribution of economic and social burdens.

It is my intention in this chapter to present a vision of the kind of economic order implicit in the concept of justice presented by liberation theologians. The argument is a soft rather than a hard one. I am arguing not that the vision presented here is *the* economic order liberation theologians advocate but rather is a vision which is not in contradiction with the concept of justice presented in the previous chapters. In considering these matters, one must necessarily allow for some latitude. The divergent historical, cultural, socioeconomic, and political factors present in the various Central and South American nations do not allow one to present a blueprint for all of them to follow. Many issues and nuances must remain within the domain of economic experts. However, my goal is to point toward the direction liberation theologians believe the economies of their countries should be moving.

Normatively speaking, liberation theologians conceive a just economic order as one in which producers and consumers, in association with each other, attempt to regulate their productive activity so that the distributive outcome as well as the process of exchange allows all members of society to achieve the good life. Society ought to be organized in ways that will allow all its members, not just the majority, to satisfy their basic biological survival, and sociocultural needs. On this basis they will be able to establish bonds of mutuality for their realization as responsible sociohistoric actors or beings of praxis. In this perspective, the ultimate purpose of economic life is not just to enable people to have more but rather to enable them to become more. Becoming a responsible political and historical agent within a communal context of equals takes precedence over merely possessing.

This normative notion of the economic order, with its implicit theological underpinnings, cannot but make us aware that ultimately every economic system stands to be improved. When seen from the perspective of an ultimate norm, all systems are and remain imperfect. However, this should not discourage our commitment to become engaged in the process of social change. It should not serve as an ideological tool for the justification of the status quo. One must not infer from the fact that the realization of our ultimate norms is likely to remain beyond our sociohistorical possibilities that we are unable to engage in a process of social transformation that can make a significant difference in the improvement of our national and international community. Given our technological development, we are now able to restructure the world economic order so as to reduce significantly the condition of extreme poverty and the state of living death in which many are forced to live. This is a task worthy of our commitment, no matter how short it falls of the ultimate ideal. If we are unable to achieve ultimate perfection, we must recognize that within history we are confronted not with ultimate perfection but with particular forms of social and historical imperfection. The imperfections are different in degree and allow themselves to be transformed and overcome through our action. We are not able to eradicate sin as such, but we seem to be able to eradicate some specific ways sin manifests itself socially. Some changes do lead to a significant improvement of our personal, communal, and collective existence. I will now examine some of the key economic issues dealt with by liberation theologians.

### The Question of Property Ownership

From a liberation perspective, a central issue concerning the question of social justice is that of the system of property ownership that defines the basic character of the economic order. Two reasons arise as to why this issue receives priority of consideration. First, it is the main question involved in the option for socialism. Socialism, regardless of the different ways we may conceive it, is always defined as a particular form of property ownership. That socioeconomic order attempts to abolish or significantly reduce private ownership of the social means of production and increase communal and/or state ownership over the main centers of production. Second, and what is more significant, the institution of property determines the possibilities and limits of the distribution of economic goods and social services. It has much bearing on the determination of what, how, and for whom social goods and services will be produced and how they can and will be distributed.

An economic order is a complex but still unified totality that demands that all its variables, particularly the process of production and distribution, be harmonious and congruent with each other. This is necessary for the functioning and the preservation of every economic order. The production and distribution processes cannot be viewed as isolated and independent variables. They must be seen as correlated and codetermined. One cannot, for example, focus exclusively on maximizing production and assume that by efficiently allocating resources and increasing the amount of social goods and services, the issue of achieving a just distribution of what has

been produced will automatically be solved. There is no arguing against the fact that available social goods and services have
to be increased if one is to enhance the possibility for social
justice. A fair distribution under conditions of extreme scarcity
can only lead to the universalization of the condition of pauper-
ism. Production must increase but it must do so in ways that do
not allow the maximization of goods and services to lead at one
and the same time toward extreme social inequality as has been
the experience of Central and South American countries.[1]

The distribution of available social goods and services, thus,
cannot be determined at will nor exclusively on the basis of
moral or religious principles. It has to take into account the way
society has organized its process of production. Policies of distribution cannot encourage practices that would go against, or
seriously undermine, the particular way the economic order
has been institutionalized. Any attempt to forward policies of
distribution that contradict the limits imposed by the way the
economic system has been organized to produce is likely to
create uncertainty and frustration among the members of society and thus general social instability. They are likely to be
perceived as arbitrary violations of the reasonable expectations
citizens have formed on the basis of the way the economic order
is organized, not just structurally but also ideologically. If
pushed to the limit, such distributive policies could discourage
the incentive to produce and initiate a period of economic
crisis.

Given the intrinsic interconnection that exists between the
process of production and the distributive process, the goal of
creating a more egalitarian national and international economic order demands much more than merely reforming the
distributive procedures of the present world capitalist system.
It demands the abrogation of the way wealth is accumulated
and distributed within the capitalist framework. Thus it demands the abrogation of capitalism itself and of the institution
of private property over the social means of production that
defines this economic order. This is why for liberation theolo-

gians the question of private ownership receives priority in their consideration of social justice.

The struggle for social justice within a liberation perspective takes place in the context of the struggle toward the abolition of private ownership of the social means of production. It attempts to resolve the basic contradiction that while all members of society participate in the productive process only a few have ownership and control over the goods and services that have been socially produced, forming the foundation for the division of society into social classes whose interests are not just contradictory but also antagonistic. Ownership of great masses of capital inevitably leads to a concentration of wealth and power that enables owners to assert their interest and power, at times, even against the well-being of society as a whole. Only sheer force can sustain an economic order "beyond the time of its ability to provide for the basic needs of all mankind and to organize the productive forces of man and his technological discoveries in such a way that all men may realize their creative potentialities."[2]

Extreme inequality in wealth and power distorts the relationships between social classes. They tend to become relationships of domination and exploitation—the few are able to appropriate the work of the many and use it for the fulfillment of their narrow self-interest. They also have more leverage when it is time to negotiate contracts in which salary and working conditions are established.[3] Owners keep for themselves the power to decide what to produce, how and for whom, who will and will not work, what technology to use and at what rate, what to reinvest and where, and what to consume. They have virtually a monopoly over the decision-making process and make decisions in terms of their narrow self-interest. Business owners, with or without intention, end up having control both over the world of things and people.

Nonowners, on the other hand, can become so dependent and powerless that they are in danger of becoming nothing more than animated tools whose life purpose is limited to attending and serving the interests of the powerful. Their capacity to produce a profit, or serve in some capacity the lifestyle of the rich and powerful, is what will ultimately determine whether or not they will be able to sustain their own life. Within many Central and South American nations where there are no strong labor and peasant movements and where there is a huge marginal population, owners of capital-land are perceived as having the power of life and death. This perception is not completely wrong.

The dehumanizing experience of masses of people dying before their time, unable to satisfy their basic biological needs, much less to realize their potential as sociocultural creatures, all because the logic of capitalist accumulation requires it, has led liberation theologians and the social movements to opt for socialism as an alternative way to accumulate and distribute wealth. Thus, the option for socialism is grounded in the lived experience of the systematic and consistent denial of the right to well-being, i.e., the denial of goods and services necessary for the preservation of life.[4]

Socialism as the negation and resolution of the contradiction of capitalist accumulation and distribution must strive to achieve at least three things: collective ownership of the social means of production and the assurance that all members of society have access to the instruments of work; that producers be able to appropriate—directly or indirectly—what they have produced; and that producers have a voice in the economic centers of decision making which have a significant effect over their individual and collective lives. From a liberation perspective, justice talk has little meaning if it does not concern itself with a more egalitarian distribution of social wealth and power.

Social appropriation, control, and regulation of the social means of production mean state ownership. Other forms of social and collective ownership, such as syndicate control over some sectors of the economy, cooperatives of consumers and producers, and municipal ownership of the industry of a town, do not constitute in themselves socialist ownership. These are creative and legitimate ways of broadening popular participation and control over sectors of the economy. Within a socialist regime creative forms of ownership ought to be encouraged as a way of strengthening the social consciousness and behavior of citizens. Still, in terms of the social interest these economic arrangements represent, they are too particular, too focused on the interest of a limited constituency. Unfortunately syndicate control, cooperatives, and municipal ownerships are not able to make the common good, the good of society as a whole, their primary concern. As they exist presently in many Central and South American nations, they attempt to counterbalance the individualistic and egoistic tendencies present within the capitalist ethos. They are attempts at reforming the capitalist economic system without challenging the chronic structural problems inherent within it. Ultimately, community forms of ownership attempt to make the system more palatable to a sector of the lower middle class so that the wealthy can continue to consolidate their privileged position.

From a liberation perspective, the state is perceived as the institution that has the responsibility of protecting and forwarding the common good. Being the most inclusive institution of society, the state has the responsibility to see to it that each person's right to well-being is fulfilled. To protect each citizen's right to well-being the state must assume control of those forms of economic activity that are so essential to the life of society. If left in the hands of private owners, they would enjoy undue power over others. No person or social group should control resources and power that can affect society as a whole. One of the goals of socializing property is in fact to increase the number of property owners. The expropriation of the instruments of work by the state, i.e., the transfer of private ownership into public ownership, is done for the sake of broadening ownership. It is to assure producers that they will in fact be able to appropriate what they have produced. Liberation theologians seem to recognize in the act of production a moral foundation for property ownership. Since no individual alone produces great masses of capital, nor the social instruments of work, no legitimate claims can be made for private ownership. Rather they are produced from our collective efforts, thus they should be collectively owned.

There is no natural or human right to ownership of the social means of production. Capitalist forms of ownership are neither natural nor the only human way of organizing property relationships. It is an economic system that has resulted from social convention within given sociohistorical circumstances, attempting to solve particular economic problems. As such, capitalism has no claim to eternity. It too must give way to other economic configurations capable of solving some of the economic problems capitalism itself has created and is not able to solve.

From a liberation perspective, private possession in general is not really a right; it is more a privilege granted by society under specific sociohistorical circumstances. Human rights and social justice demand not so much ownership over the social instruments of work but rather that citizens have access to the instruments of work and ownership over the fruits of their labor. Ownership is secondary to having access and being capable of using the social instruments of work. The prior right is the right to use. Ownership should be directed toward a management and administration that seeks to assure all people within the community the right to use the instruments necessary to sustain and forward their life.[5]

Even within socialism, however, there is recognition of the need for particular forms of private ownership, and thus, of the legitimacy of certain forms of property ownership. One must have property rights if one is to have an autonomous and purposeful life. Socialism denies us the right to have ownership over the social means of production in order to guarantee us the right of ownership over those durable and nondurable consumer goods that are necessary if we are to realize our potentialities and carry out our self-given life plans. These forms of ownership free us from being dependent on others, including the state. They seek to assure us of a personal and public space in which we can act with autonomy and exercise our responsibility. Thus, they provide us with a sense of social stability, identity, and personal worth.

Socialism is based on the presupposition that the social instruments of work must be collectively owned. Any attempt to allow private ownership over a significant sector of the economy must bear the burden of proof. Its necessity and advantages must be argued. Within a socialist framework, thus, there exists the possibility of allowing space for the existence of small private forms of capitalist ownership. If, for example, it can be shown that: (a) government ownership and management of small industries or land holdings is inefficient and in fact reduces the level of productivity; (b) private ownership and enterprise in these areas can improve the level of well-being of the region; (c) the number of workers employed is small, and by and large benefit from this arrangement; or (d) these forms of enterprise abide by the established norms and do not violate the goals of solidarity, fraternity, and the sense of the common good, then it seems sound, economically speaking, to allow and even encourage such islands of private ownership to emerge.

The existence of small islands of private ownership could very well have beneficial results for society as a whole. They could generate a competition toward efficient production, encourage private initiative and creativity, and increase the general level of production in a context in which no one is risking their means of livelihood. It is important that the inevitable inequalities that are likely to emerge from this arrangement be limited and regulated so that they do not allow some members of society to have the capacity to dominate and exploit others. Inequalities of wealth and power among the members of society will always be, but a politically regulated society can prevent some from subjugating others.

How much and to what extent private ownership should be allowed is a matter of social convention and political wisdom, an issue for the community as a whole to decide and evaluate. The transition from capitalism to socialism will also be conditioned by the particular socioeconomic and political circumstances of the country in question, and even by the international power struggle. As the process of socialization takes place, we must always be aware of the human cost involved in every process of deep social change, and we must minimalize this. From a liberation perspective it is clear that the transformation of the economic structure of society, no matter how radical, will not bring with it the eradication of all the distortions present in our mutual relationships. There are political, social, cultural, and psychological dimensions to the various ways humans exploit and dominate each other. A change within the economic structure will not in itself bring changes at these other levels. The experience of sixty-seven years of socialism in different countries speaks both to the possibilities and limits of sociostructural change. Nonetheless, if inequalities of property and income, and the social antagonism based on these, are to be significantly reduced, the capitalist mode of accumulating wealth and allocating and distributing resources must be replaced by a socialist mode of production and distribution.

While the abolition of private ownership of the social means of production is a necessary condition for the creation of a socialist regime, it is still not a sufficient condition. Socialism also implies the abolition of mercantilist forms of production and distribution, i.e., production, organized in terms of the profit motive, that gives priority to the demands of those who can afford to have their needs met and that distributes goods and services by some desert criterion such as contribution, merit, or effort. Mercantile relationships, in which human needs are subordinated to many other economic considerations, can exist outside capitalism. It is only when the social division of labor is organized with the purpose of satisfying the life-needs of the members of society (as a matter of priority) and their sociocultural needs and when the criterion of need becomes the content of justice that we can meaningfully speak of socialism.

In short, within the liberation perspective there is room for a variety of forms of property organization and ownership. This is instrumental in forwarding the creativity and responsibility of citizens as well as for maximizing production in an efficient and just way. Large scale industry, with its complex organization and technology, must be state-run and managed. Their impact on society as a whole and the need society has of them is too great to allow local managers and workers to have decision-making power. The common good is at stake. This makes it the responsibility of the state. In other industries where the good of society as a whole is not at stake, managers, workers, and consumers must have more autonomy in deciding how and what to produce and thus more control over the decision-making process, although some state presence and coordination is necessary. Smaller economic units can be created and managed with even greater autonomy by cooperatives, municipal ownership, and syndicates. The prevailing system of law will be the medium which keeps them within the limits of the ethos of welfare that informs the social order. Finally, small private ownership and even individual initiative can exist. One can do well while contributing by providing goods and services demanded by society that are not supplied by other sectors of the economy.

It is essential that citizens have an active voice in the decision-making process—deciding what kinds of private ownership are to be encouraged and tolerated, what forms of manager, worker, and consumer participation are desirable. These choices are very much part of the process by which a community develops and asserts its identity as citizens. Only by experimenting, learning by mistakes, and bringing creative and imaginative solutions to problems do people become effective economic agents, beings of praxis.

## Economic Democracy

From a liberation perspective, capitalism is an economic order that is intrinsically undemocratic. It excludes producers and workers from the main centers of economic policy making where all important decisions regarding economic life are made. Capitalism is the power to decide what owners are unlikely to give up and what they will struggle the hardest to keep![6] Workers and producers are confined to performing assigned roles decided by others on the basis of their concept of what is proper. This represents a serious limitation of the workers' possibilities for actualizing themselves as beings of praxis.

If the new socialist regime is to avoid having an economic elite replaced by a political elite and an economic hierarchy by a political hierarchy, it must find ways of effectively subjecting the economic system to public control. It must establish an economic democracy that assures all social members the right to participate in the centers of economic decision making. The right of access to the instruments of work seeks among other things to empower people so that they can effectively become responsible social agents with the ability to participate in the regulation of all social institutions that have a significant influence in their lives. Ultimately property truly belongs to those who have a voice in the process by which decisions are made about what to do with it. Social appropriation, thus, goes hand in hand with social participation.

An economic order is very much a manifestation of social power. For such power to be exercised legitimately and responsibly it must be based on the consent of those it affects. When people are deprived of having a say in the economic centers of decision making, their right to life can be more easily disregarded and violated. Some assume the power to decide whether or not others will work. Whenever a sector of society is incapable of asserting its views and interest, it can easily be disregarded. This is true both in the political and the economic realm. Thus, the importance of having some form of access to the economic centers of decision making is paramount. If one's needs must be attended so as to empower one to become politically active, it is equally true that one must be politically active to see to it that one's needs are attended. If people are going to be the authors of their own liberation, they must participate at this level as well. José Porfirio Miranda makes this point clear in his denunciation of one of the shortcomings of the Mexican revolution:

> It [the revolution] believed that justice consisted solely in equi-
> table forms of distribution, overlooking the fact that the same
> sense of justice demands, with even greater urgency, that the
> people themselves be the authors of their own uplifting and
> betterment; with this omission, which made the people into
> objects rather than subjects of the revolution, the revolution
> found itself deprived of the force necessary to effect equitable
> forms of distribution before the resistance of an ever more
> powerful capitalism.[7]

Developmentalism as a model of development is rejected
by liberation theologians precisely because it offers strictly
technological and technocratic solutions to the problems of national development—the solutions of experts and elites in the
absence of broad popular participation. This model of development minimizes the importance of popular participation and in
particular the empowerment of the poor as intrinsic to the
process of socioeconomic development. At best, it promises the
people that they will be able to consume more, particularly if
they follow the prescriptions of experts and abandon their political involvements and demands. Political movements are seen
as contradicting economic development. Developmentalists
argue that people will have more if they surrender their desire
to become effective historical actors. From a liberation perspective, this process must be reversed, the empowerment of the
people, in particular the poor, has priority. The use and application of technology is made in the context of the cultural revolution.

It is at the workplace that we spend most of our life activity.
Thus it is crucial that producers understand the dynamics and
participate actively at this level that is so central to their existence. Their participation will assure that production will in fact
be carried out to attend to basic needs, appropriating collectively what they cannot appropriate individually. The democra-
tization of the economy is a way of creating a system of checks
and balances that can mitigate the overconcentration of power
that occurs when the state becomes the center of both economic and political power. If we are to avoid an economic elite
being replaced by a political elite, then it is important that the

economic order be democratized. Decision makers in both the political and economic realms must always be made responsive to the needs of those they are called to serve. They must also be freed from the temptation of seeking more power and benefits for themselves and those they favor than what they are entitled to. They must be reminded that they are literally public servants. Ultimately, popular participation is required in any economic system which claims to be just since a person cannot be reduced to a mere executor of another's decisions.

The process of establishing an economic democracy must take into account the issue of efficiency in the production of goods and services. This has always been a serious problem in the creation and establishment of socialist regimes. The productive process of nations moving rapidly toward industrialization is extremely complex. The technological apparatus that is used and the management and skills required to make it function properly demand knowledge and skills beyond those of the average citizen. Undifferentiated participation can prove to be not only economically inefficient but also unjust. To demand from people responsibilities and entrust them with tasks they are not trained for and/or do not fully understand can prove damaging to a person's sense of worth and self-respect, as well as harmful for society as a whole. There are limits to the form and extent of popular participation. The need that sophisticated economic orders have to establish long-term plans, plans that cannot be easily changed, limits the way economic democracy can be institutionalized.

The view that only the talented, skilled, and trained should manage and decide in matters pertaining to economic development does have some merit. The learned must be entrusted with the responsibility of organizing the economy to assure the common good. Still, one must recognize that the best and the brightest need to be reminded of their accountability to the community at large. One must also recognize that the establishment of priorities between the democratic principle and the principle of efficient production is itself a political decision that the citizen must make, since it is not clear that one necessarily must always have priority over the other. Finally, one must also recognize that if it is true that the drive toward economic democracy can at times contradict the quest for efficient production, this is not always the case. Popular participation is not necessarily antagonistic to efficient production.

Both humanly constructive and economically efficient ways to enhance popular participation can be found. For one, producers, workers, and consumer groups can participate in the election of managers, technicians, and other skilled personnel who can do the job well. They can also create councils where the experts come and give account of what they are doing. In those areas where workers themselves manage, they should have greater control. Producer, consumer, and worker councils should also exist and have an independent voice within governmental agencies whose responsibility is to make decisions regarding the economic destiny of the nation. These and other forms of enhancing popular participation in economic matters enable the people to have a more refined understanding of the economic order.

For liberation theologians, economic liberation is not only freedom from material need but also freedom to develop one's potential fully. It demands that we have control over those aspects of life which affect us in a significant way.[8]

The human within us is realized from within by means of our sociohistorical action. A just economic order in the process of enhancing broad popular participation must also foster the emergence of elitist elements within the rank and file of workers and producers. These elitist elements are the people of vision, conscience, and commitment that embody the values and aspirations of their peers and take responsibility for developing the skills and knowledge to perform their tasks well. They are also people with a strong sense of calling and vocation to public service, in particular a sense of serving the poor. Such people deserve the privilege of holding positions of power and prestige. It is within this sphere that the criterion of merit is a valid and relevant criterion of distribution.

Economic democracy, far from being an obstacle to efficient production, can itself become an incentive to maximize and make more efficient social productivity. When the process of production is collectively administered, when workers and producers are integrated into the decision-making process, it is not unreasonable to think that their newly acquired sense of the role their labor plays in fulfilling social needs can give them a new sense of meaning. Their labor and their activity is seen in a new light as having more worth than the salary they receive for it. Work becomes a task meaningful and valuable in itself, its own incentive. This new vision of work can become part of an incentive structure that commits workers to produce to the best of their ability and to become more efficient in whatever they do.

This is not to say that material incentives are completely eliminated or replaced by moral incentives or social recognition. Material reward is the mode of incentive that accounts for much of capitalism's capacity to produce, renovate, and invent. It is clear to liberation theologians that material incentives, in the form of difference in income, can contribute both to one's own personal development and to the well-being of society. In principle nothing is wrong with allowing salary differences. They can be useful as well as just. Differences in wealth and power are an intrinsic part of social life. When material reward is used to elicit from free agents their efforts in the production of goods or services needed by the community—significantly reducing the need to have some people assign others to perform jobs which they find unattractive—nothing is wrong with it.[9]

## The Right to Work

For liberation theologians "first comes the right to work and all other rights are mediated through it."[10] Work is at the center of those activities that enable us to realize ourselves as beings of praxis. It is intrinsic to the right to well-being and, thus, to the realization of social justice. That persons as persons have a right to be employed and to derive from it what they need to live with dignity places the political community under the obligation to provide each of its members with work. It is part of what gives legitimacy to a political community. A just economic order and a just process of development is one that gives priority to the people's right to work. Particularly within poor nations, it is essential that the state avoid the underutilization of its most precious resource: the work of its people.

A society capable of feeding and caring for all its members but which denies a significant sector of it the possibility of working is unjust.[11] Welfare compensation is no substitute for work and for the sense of self-respect, dignity, and security it entails. People are entitled first of all to become agents, not just recipients of the productivity of others. Persons capable of working find it demeaning to live off the efforts of others. To do so reinforces a sense of false dependence and makes people oblivious to their own creative capabilities. Society has an obligation to provide all its members with work. They in turn have an obligation to produce to the best of their efforts so they not only realize their potentialities but also contribute to the realization of the potentialities of other members of society.

One way, of course, citizens do contribute so that others can become creative agents is by establishing a social welfare system whose purpose is to provide those left out of the economic system with the goods and services they need. This is part of every citizen's obligation and part of his or her contribution to the common good. Still, the welfare system is no substitute for the obligation the state has of providing work for all adults able to work. Welfare ought to be a system of temporary aid, not a way of life for future generations, usually generations of the same social class.

As conditions permit, persons ought to be able to choose their work freely. Society must attempt to create conditions for its members to develop their potentialities. Work must be chosen because it fulfills a person's inner-felt need, corresponding to his or her sense of vocation. Much has been said of the frustration that comes from making a choice for a given profession on the basis of the economic security and social prestige it brings, rather than on one's vocational preference. This has a detrimental effect on the producer's incentive to perform to the best of her or his ability.

Clearly every economic order requires that certain tasks that are in themselves nonfulfilling must be performed. These are physically taxing, unpleasant, repetitious, and monotonous jobs that do not enable anyone to find in them an incentive for their performance. A just distribution of these social burdens must also be enacted. As far as possible, they should be widely distributed among members of society. They must be generously compensated and those engaged in them should enjoy enough leisure so as to become engaged in other more meaningful and humanly rewarding activities.

Justice, defined as distribution according to need, rests on the prior or more basic notion that all persons as persons are equal in dignity and as such are entitled to equal consideration and regard in respect to the claims they make over these goods and services they need to fulfill their life plans. All members of society are equally entitled to what they need to live a life worthy of the name human. Considerations of merit at this level have no bearing since no one is entitled to his or her life more than another. Merit and desert are recognized as valid criteria of justice, but their sphere must be limited to make visible in all social spheres equal respect for all persons.

Regarding the preservation of life, which is the main concern of social justice, the criterion of merit is not relevant: persons as persons are entitled to it equally. The criterion of merit is very relevant in the sphere of criminal justice, where merit or desert must be clearly shown before one pronounces punishment. Only a criminal deed deserves to be punished. In the process of giving prizes and rewarding the winners of a competition, the criterion of desert is also relevant. Even in the distribution of offices, what a person has or has not done is a relevant criterion in establishing whether or not that person deserves what is given to her or him.

Liberation theologians argue against the meritarian conception of justice that is intrinsic to capitalism and the market distribution mechanism. They denounce the inordinate inequalities of wealth and power that this economic system not only tolerates but even encourages so as to assure maximum and efficient productivity. These inequalities are perceived by them as a practical denial of the sense of human dignity, a violation of the principle of equality that is intrinsic to the notion of social justice.

They also reject the priorities of the marketplace. From their point of view, the market mechanism gives priority to individual needs and wants over social and communal needs. It tends to give priority to the needs and wants of the wealthy and powerful over the needs and wants of the poor and powerless. The market gives preferential treatment to those who have resources to compete for the goods and services it provides. As long as they are able to pay, the market will produce for them. The market does not concern itself with and is unable to measure what the community as a whole would like to have in terms of jobs, housing, education, health services, and so on. Those who have little or no resources and who cannot become contenders in the supply-demand power struggle of the market are not perceived as having needs or wants. A nonprofitable need or want is not recognized as a legitimate need or want.

Within poor nations this is somewhat more evident than within wealthy ones. Many of these weaker economies in fact spend a significant part of their productive effort and resources in the production of leisure and luxury goods demanded by the rich rather than in life-sustaining goods and services needed by the poor, who are the majority of the population. The market allows a few to squander resources to satisfy their wants and desires in the midst of extreme poverty where many do not even have what they need to survive. Within the market, there is in fact no effort made to differentiate among wants, needs, and preferences.

From a liberation perspective there is something intrinsically unjust about an economic system that allows procedural concerns to prevail regardless of the consequences and that equalizes all values to a quantitative measure. Economic categories and procedures must be subordinated to normative criteria, criteria decided politically by the community, taking into account the consequences of procedures and policies.

When need is made the main criterion of social justice, one must attempt to arrive at some understanding of what constitutes a legitimate need claim. One must also try to establish some form for determining priorities among the different needs the community has.

Every political community is a gathering of people with a plurality of needs. It is extremely difficult, given the competing claims, to determine a normative theory of needs that provides criteria and procedures to distinguish among needs and order them in ways acceptable to all members of society. It is likely that there will always be disagreement among the members of society regarding this issue. Although there might never be an objective and universally acceptable theory of need, it is still necessary to have a theory which at least appears reasonable.

Liberation theologians seem to uphold a theory of human needs, dividing them into two main categories: biological and sociocultural needs. A third category is not needs proper but wants, desires, or preferences that can properly be called luxury or status "needs." The first two categories are grounded in our biological and sociocultural existence. They include goods and services necessary for the preservation of our existence as well as those necessary to develop our potentialities as sociocultural beings and to carry out whatever purposes we identify as worthy of our commitments. The former sustain our life; the latter enable us to experience purpose and meaning, that is, to develop as free and responsible agents. Any economic system that is just must give priority to and seek to attend to these needs for all its members and within its possibilities contribute so that other political communities can do the same.

Human needs must be fulfilled if a person is not to be injured in a fundamental way. They must be attended to if persons are to realize themselves as beings of praxis. They enable persons to develop life plans and to have a meaningful say in the realization of their common destinies.

Luxury or status needs, on the other hand, are not, properly speaking, human needs, in that they are not essential for persons to be able to realize themselves as free and responsible human agents. If luxury needs are not satisfied, no harm is done in any morally significant way. It would not prevent people from formulating and realizing their self-given life plans or hinder them from being responsible agents in the process of transforming their sociocultural world. These are needs that are essentially external to the morally serious purposes a person or a community give themselves.

Luxury or status needs are derivative and of secondary importance. They are more a matter of privilege and social convention than a right or a matter of justice. Being secondary does not mean that they have no place or value. People might very well be entitled to these goods and services but only after the basic needs of the members of society have been met. While there exist masses of people whose most basic needs have not been fulfilled, it is a violation of our religious heritage and of basic human dignity to give priority to the production and consumption of these goods and services.

From a liberation perspective, a reasonable criterion for determining legitimate needs is found by looking at the life plans of persons and their communities. It is assumed in this view that a person's needs and those of the community he or she belongs to are not infinite but more or less capable of being defined and limited. Persons are seen as needing work and the sustenance, security, and independence it provides. They also need to belong to a community that provides them with the goods and services to realize their potentialities as well as a sense of belonging and social identity which is itself part of what constitutes a good life. Finally, they need the freedom to engage in creative-inventive activity. These are the basic dimensions which are necessary for people to be able to have a purposeful life. The political community needs to be able to assert its cultural identity, formulate and carry out its collective purposes, and achieve security and autonomy before other nations. Communities and individuals may want and desire many things but they are only entitled, as a matter of justice, to what they need to be able to realize their self-given life plans.

The process of dependent development Central and South American nations have been forced to live under has not allowed them to produce the goods and services necessary to attend to the needs of the majority of their people. In the short run not even a socialist revolution will be able to produce goods and services necessary for all members of society to become equally fulfilled participants. Liberation theologians, however, seem convinced that a popular socialist regime will be able to abolish quite rapidly those dehumanizing forms of poverty that have plagued their nations. While abundance seems far away, the goal for people to experience a more humane life can be achieved for all members of society.

Socialism provides for these nations an alternative and viable way of engaging in a process of sustained economic development and promises the establishment of a new economic ethos, one which is very much in tune with the aspirations and religious values of their culture. It is an ethos in which people live not in order to have but have in order to live with others in community for the sake of their mutual well-being. It is an ethos that, while calling the people to celebrate life, also makes them conscious of the place and need for austerity and sacrifice in the process of forwarding social justice. Creativity and celebration in this context become much more than pleasure seeking, and austerity and sacrifice are no longer adaptations to conditions of exploitation and domination in which the weak are coerced to accept the artificial scarcity the wealthy and powerful force upon them. Creativity and celebration are now discovered in the process of empowering the poor and marginal to become active social participants.

Poor nations, in their attempt to allow their people to reappropriate control over their destiny, can and should nationalize and expropriate all foreign investments that infringe on the nation-state's capacity to exercise and preserve its sovereignty. The state must have control over the main national sources of wealth and power. A state that has control over its resources and that can assert its sovereignty can in turn have the freedom to encourage foreign investment and even allow for foreign ownership of sectors of the national economy without being threatened.

A strong and independent nation-state is also necessary to create conditions for the practice of mutuality among nations. A relatively equal capacity among nations to exercise their sovereignty creates conditions for mutual development and growth. It is becoming increasingly clear that nations need each other for their mutual well-being and humanization. Thus, it is essential that relationships of domination and exploitation be overcome. In today's world, isolationism can only bring mutual impoverishment, which would be felt most strongly among poor nations.

Mutuality at the international level demands that wealthy nations share their resources and technical expertise with poor nations in nonpaternalistic ways, that is, by carefully listening to the needs and expectations of the poor. On this basis, it makes sense to demand from poor nations that they too sacrifice and practice austerity. Sacrifice and austerity can be voluntarily accepted by a people when they recognize others, for the sake of forwarding the common good, doing so as well. One cannot expect poor nations to accept sacrifices while the wealthy continue to squander resources. The road toward international and global solidarity demands mutual commitment and sharing in both the benefits and sacrifices implied in this historical project. The time for global economic planning is near. It is becoming a necessity, not just for achieving global justice, but for the possibility of human survival.[12]

At both the national and international level, the criterion of need ought to govern the production and distribution of social goods and services. Nations have an obligation to attend to the needs of their own citizens. As conditions permit, they also have an obligation to help other nations arrive at conditions in which they might be able to do the same. Social and global justice demand that extreme forms of inequality in wealth and power be eliminated and that wealth and power be placed at the service of the poorest sectors of society and the world.

## Egalitarianism

To give to each according to his or her need seems to contradict the aims of equality. After all, different persons have different needs. Even those that have similar needs require different amounts of resources to satisfy them. The criterion of need, although it strives to create equality, does not strive to achieve sameness. In attempting to satisfy the needs of different individuals it seeks to forward the plurality of talents, skills, and abilities that make social life possible and humanly rewarding. An egalitarian society does not seek the same quality of life for all its members but seeks to assure all its members the possibility of obtaining that good life of which they are capable. In not denying anyone the right to well-being it strives for the equal dignity of all humans as humans. The recognition of this morally significant equality is what an egalitarian society seeks to preserve and forward for all its members. Theologically speaking, it has to do with being a child of God and a sister or brother to humanity.

Persons are not equally talented, skilled, prudent, intelligent, nor do they have the same dispositions or abilities. An egalitarian society recognizes and encourages such differences as a way of enabling each person to develop his or her potentialities to the fullest. It denounces as unjust any attempt to equalize the talented to the less talented. It also recognizes the fundamental injustice of demanding from the less talented what is beyond them. These are both equally wasteful and oppressive. It will always be the case that some will have more capacity to live a creative and rewarding life. However, since all humans have talents and abilities, it is equally important to recognize the obligation to attend to their claims so that they too are satisfied. Their claims must be given equal consideration.

An egalitarian social order encourages and preserves differences and talents among its members but seeks to avoid having these become the opportunity for some people to exploit and dominate others. Thus, it tries to keep differences within limits so that in our mutual sociopolitical and personal dealings we never lose sight of the equal dignity of every person.

From a liberation perspective neither Scripture nor the Christian tradition provide, by themselves, enough resources from which to deduce what the just economic order is and how to structure it. Those inclined to argue that their options are in fact based on the prescriptions of Scripture are seen as trying either to sacralize the status quo or the alternative option they uphold to replace it. Such attempts border on idolatry. However, if one cannot argue that one's alternative sociopolitical option is the one derived from Scripture and/or the Christian tradition, one can still argue that one's option is not in contradiction with the tradition and with what Scripture presents as being within the parameters of God's purpose for humanity. The community of faith always seeks to inform its thinking and acting in light of the wisdom of tradition and Scripture.

Liberation theologians argue that God's creation is good. It is the foundation of all that nourishes and sustains life, in particular human life. God alone has ultimate ownership of all that is and all that is must be placed at the service of God's life-sustaining purpose. Legitimate ownership makes one a steward of God, placing one in a special obligation to use one's resources and talents to attend to the needs and increase the freedom of those who are in need. As God's children we are all equally entitled to ownership, and we have an obligation to see that in fact all people have their needs attended. Being in possession of goods and services that others need to achieve their well-being places us under the obligation to attend to their needs. We are called to find both personal and political means of meeting this obligation.

God calls us as a people. Communal existence is intrinsic to the divine promise of Shalom. God creates community especially where there seems to be neither subjective nor objective conditions for it. God is a God who dwells at the margin among the poor and powerless and within them manifests the divine as the power to sustain and nourish life. We encounter God where God calls us to encounter Deity in the process of creating life-sustaining community among the poor and powerless. It is in this context that we are called to love one another, to strive toward more inclusiveness so that all are able to experience the good life of which we are capable. For the community of faith, love in the form of service to others is intrinsic to the good life. This is why the concept of justice in our religious tradition is more radical and demanding than that of our sociopolitical heritage. It calls us to attend to the needs of the weak and poor just because they have the need and we have the services and goods necessary to satisfy that need. Whether or not we are or have been responsible for their present condition is irrelevant.

Acts of community building and life-sustaining practice have meaning beyond the immediate well-being of humanity. It is a way of anticipating and experiencing God's kingdom of peace and justice. It is a way of participating in God's continuing creation. God is a God of order and regularity, order and regularity within nature. Society and the larger realm of history enable us to enjoy a good life. But God is also a God of newness and new beginnings. God is experienced as the Creator of new possibilities, of temporary chaos that renews and enhances our life experiences. This experience of God is basic to the community of faith that commits itself to the process of liberation.

# 5

# POLITICAL JUSTICE

•

The term *liberation* points to "the priority of the political with its basic reference to the socioeconomic realm."[1] The struggle for social justice is primarily a political struggle since the creation of a just economic order is dependent on the capacity workers and peasants have to take control of the state. This is the only way they will be able to assert their class interest and begin to realize their historical project of creating a more egalitarian society.

The political has primacy in that at the very least it determines the formal order of all other social institutions, affecting all levels of social life. The state does not have to dictate the precise nature and limits of the activities carried out by other social institutions, although such is the practice of totalitarian states. But the state does organize and regulate all social institutions into a coherent whole.

The political also has primacy in that it is the realm in which people come together to decide how they will organize their collective existence. The way society can organize itself is very much determined by its present socioeconomic stage of development. Still, the particular form the social order will take is not dictated by the socioeconomic stage of development but rather is decided politically. The selection of the economic system itself is a political decision, as are matters pertaining to the technological, social, and cultural aspects of life.

No realm escapes being influenced by the political. The political is so embracing that it affects, if only indirectly, even the most private dimensions of our existence. Thus, from a liberation perspective human action is necessarily political.

We cannot achieve a correct understanding of human existence if we proceed by compartmentalizing it into mutually exclusive and discretely defined realms. Such a procedure tends to lead to dualistic understandings of the human which tend to be conservative and even reactionary. The insistence upon establishing radical dichotomies between the different realms of human existence also encourages attitudes of complacency, resignation, and indifference toward the political reality lived by the poor and powerless. They make us oblivious to the complexity of the real and concrete conditions under which human life unfolds.

From a liberation perspective, it is imperative and urgent that we politicize human consciousness by integrating all sectors of society into the political arena. This is particularly important for the poor and marginal and their historical project of liberation. Thus, Gutiérrez insists "on a society in which, by appropriating the means of production, the masses appropriate their own political management as well, and definitive freedom, thereby occasioning the creation of a new social consciousness."[2] It is in the political realm that people discover themselves as free and responsible agents, capable of taking hold of the reins of their own destiny. It is in this process, more than in any other one, that we discover ourselves as beings who are capable of responsible moral choices and actions, as beings of praxis.

Political life has an intrinsically moral dimension. It is that form of human practice in which people come together to debate and persuade each other as to the best ways to organize their common existence and solve the inevitable problems that are part of social life. Living in society always entails conflicts between its members. The elimination of certain sources of tension will always bring the emergence of new ones. Struggle and strife are part of social existence. They are even one of its positive aspects since, on the basis of conflicts, we create and initiate new forms of thinking and action. The political is the realm of words and deeds. The just political order is one in which the state attempts in a conscious and premeditated way to create institutions that assist its citizens to develop the virtues of rational discourse, argumentation, persuasion, and political organization—the means by which citizens can attempt to order and carry out their social life.

The state is the social instrument that has a monopoly over the social instruments of violence and the authority to use them to enforce laws and social patterns of behavior. It is not only efficient but also morally justifiable that the state have this monopoly. It would indeed be a brutish form of life if individuals were left to themselves to determine punishment and execute it. A more or less centralized power that can enforce compliance with the laws, punish violators, and keep citizens within a reasonable degree of social order makes social life both possible and worthwhile.

Still, the force and violence monopolized by the state can only be auxiliary and secondary to the preservation and day-to-day functioning of the political community. Force and violence should not become the determining elements that bond the sociopolitical community. They ought not become the basis for policy making, or for political consent, or even the sole basis for citizens to comply with the laws. When the threat of force and violence does become the sustaining ground of a social order, as is increasingly happening in most Central and South American nations, political life decays. Within these societies, described by many as ruled by institutional violence, it is impossible for political existence to be lived and experienced by words and deeds.

Within more and more of these nations all radical and even moderate attempts by workers and peasants to become effective political agents with their own historical projects are systematically and violently repressed. This has, in itself, become a painful educational experience in the conflictual nature of sociopolitical life within poor nations. Persuasion and argumentation are very limited in their ability to achieve fundamental social change, and the powerful use the terms *freedom, justice, reconciliation,* and *peace*—political terms that express the innermost longings of the community at large, in particular, the hopes of the poor—in ideological, distorted, and manipulative ways. They have learned that if the terms are to have any existential meaning, then it is indispensable that they be understood within the framework of the struggle for liberation.

The political repression experienced by workers and peasants, together with those who struggle with them, has made them develop a sense of political realism which enables them to sustain their quest for the utopian elements of their historical project. Political realism has not made them cynics. Rather, it has tempered their utopian expectations and their political imaginations to include the very difficult consideration of strategy and disciplined long-range militancy that their historical project requires. Political realism has not made them surrender to the limits and possibilities defined by the present status quo. They still recognize that ultimately their sociopolitical world is a human construction and that as such it can be changed to forward human well-being. Even with the worst of circumstances, it is possible to establish more human forms of community and new ways of being human.

Political realism also has made the workers and peasants aware that along with refined social analysis and strategy, liberation movements have to find ways of responding to the violence used by their oppressors both during the revolutionary struggle as well as in the period after their victory. Historically, the oppressors have always used every means available to preserve their position of power and prestige. Class conflict and the violence it entails, however, are not seen as natural to the human condition. Violence itself can become a means for a significant reduction in the use of violence in political life. It is this reduction of violence that ultimately justifies the revolutionary process and its attempt to create both objective and subjective conditions for social reconciliation and mutuality.

In a more restrictive sense, the state has the responsibility to create and maintain social order. It accomplishes this task primarily by means of the laws it enacts which override any other rules or procedures of lesser institutions. The state and its laws have authority over all those who live within its boundaries. Without this ordering function, we could not flourish as sociopolitical beings. It is very much part of what goes into the good life. Still, order, although a good, is neither the only good nor the supreme good. It must be placed within the larger framework of justice which, politically speaking, seeks to create conditions for the community as a whole to participate actively in the determination of its destiny. When order does become the highest good of the state, there is always the danger that creative and new thinking and action will be restricted or prohibited.

Political existence has its own sphere and integrity. Within that sphere, special justice issues arise that have to be dealt with on their own terms. They cannot be reduced to psychological, social, economic, or cultural dimensions of life. Among the political justice issues liberation theologians give attention to are issues having to do with the legitimate control and exercise of political power; questions regarding the protection and advancement of political rights, i.e., the right to freedom as well as the relationship between the right to freedom and the right to well-being; and finally, questions having to do with the nature of the common good. All of these issues are dealt with within the particular sociohistorical coordinates that define their national reality.

## Democratic Socialism

*Democratic socialism* is the term that best describes the political order liberation theologians advocate and consider just. This term is plagued with ambiguities. Conceptually, it has been used to describe a variety of political models that are quite different from one another. What seems more significant and is more troublesome is that historically the struggle for socialism seems always to be at odds with the creation of political democracies and vice versa. Still, there is no better term to describe the political option presented by liberation theologians. Thus, we must look carefully at the content they give to it.

Liberation theologians are aware of both the achievements and shortcomings of the various socialist experiments that presently exist. Míguez Bonino, for example, praises the socialist movement for its capacity to significantly reduce, directly and indirectly, malnutrition, illiteracy, and premature mortality, as well as its capacity to provide the poor with shelter, health care, and education. It has proven itself to be a viable method for social change and economic, technological, and scientific development. He is also aware of the shortcomings of this new socio-economic structure. He is disturbed by the lack of "popular participation, the control of power or the ability to overcome discrimination after the revolution."[3] Liberation movements recognize that Marxism has lost some of its revolutionary ethos and fervor. Still, no serious liberation movement can disregard Marxist social analysis since it is the only radical critique of the exploitative nature of capitalist accumulation of wealth and its unjust process of distribution.

Those engaged in the struggle for liberation cannot but engage in the act of fundamental thinking that goes hand in hand with creative action. They have to look at present socialist regimes with enough suspicion and critical distance to both retrieve what is essential to the movement's ethos and free it from the distortion present in every historically embodied project. This act of critical distance must go hand in hand with the basic sense of solidarity that ought to exist between those who struggle for their freedom and well-being within radically different sociohistorical contexts. In both action and thinking, one must avoid monolithic concepts and preconceived models, and attempt to be heroic. This is not for the sake of vain originality but to meet the demands of historical realism and political efficacy.

The content liberation theologians give to the term *democratic socialism* is vague. Part of the reason for this is that they seek to be inclusive of both the theory and practice implied in this historical project. This vagueness is also an acknowledgment of the fact that the poor themselves must have more active participation in the formulation of this new social order. Finally, it is a way of expressing that the project will be redefined in the process of bringing it about, that is, as men and women concretely attempt to solve the problems they confront within the limits of their socioeconomic context. In this process, this broad concept will become clearer and more specific.

A lack of clarity in political goals does not have to translate itself into political inaction or passivity. The nature of political and historical praxis offers no guarantees that the project we begin today will be achieved as we first conceived it. In fact, we can almost be assured that given the web of human relationships that define the political realm in which our actions are confronted and redirected by the actions of others, we are able at best to achieve an approximation of what we intended. A political project, however, does demand at least a general vision of its content and direction, liberation theologians are able to provide such a vision.

The establishment of a democratic regime requires broad popular participation at the economic level. However, this is not a sufficient condition for the realization of full democracy. Broad popular participation at the political level is needed as well. There is, in this perspective, a dialectical relationship between the socioeconomic realm and the political realm. What happens at one level will have definite consequences for what takes place at the other. However, these levels must not be confused nor reduced to each other. Socioeconomic democracy can create favorable conditions for political democracy, but it is not itself political democracy. One can have democratic control at the place of work (a goal still to be achieved by most Western industrial nations) and even participate in the democratic process of one's local community and still be deprived of having an active and effective voice in matters pertaining to the nation's interest and destiny, that is, of political democracy proper.

The political realm is not merely a reflection of underlying socioeconomic interests and forces. It has its own autonomy and laws. It is that form of democratic participation that concerns the state and its government. It is prior in importance and a determining factor for the existence of all other forms of democratic participation. There is democracy proper only where there is broad popular participation at the level of state policy.

## Legitimate Use of Political Power

Politically speaking the claim that all persons as persons are equal in all morally relevant ways means that they are entitled as a matter of justice to equal political rights. These rights are more than the mere formal claim "equal treatment under the law," which ought not to be taken lightly. They imply a substantive notion of human dignity that limits the very content that can be given to the law itself. Laws themselves cannot make legitimate arbitrary formulations and establish criteria as to who are "equals."

In a sense it is easier to distribute political rights equally than it is to distribute socioeconomic goods. The former is a matter of law and constitutional rights and as such there is, in principle, no scarcity of the goods being distributed. The goods and services distributed at the socioeconomic level are always scarce and thus it is more difficult to achieve relative equality. Still there are limits to the concrete actualization of political rights, since one must make a social investment of resources that are scarce. Thus, for example, my right to freedom, which places others under the obligation not to interfere with my action, requires for its protection and realization an expenditure in police protection. Not all societies can provide the same amount of this good. Within society, not every member can be guaranteed the same amount of protection, either. Further, there are "environmental" limits as to the possibility of effectively distributing political rights. Poverty, sickness, ignorance, fear, and the like make freedom and the possession of formal political rights meaningless for those who suffer. Thus the scarcity that plagues the socioeconomic realm affects the possibility of concretely realizing our civil and political rights in a fundamental way. The former provides means which are essential to the possibility of exercising the latter.

An equal distribution of political rights is also made impossible by the internal limits of political existence. It is the nature of political life that some will rule and others will obey. This inevitably leads to a kind of political inequality, an inequality of political power which is necessary if we are to have a political existence at all. There is nothing wrong in principle with this form of inequality, particularly if it is kept within the limits that assure that those who have more power do not dominate and exploit others by its use. Still, since the principle of political equality implies that no one has the right to govern others, this form of inequality must be justified.

The bestowal of political power must be based on some form of consent of those who are affected by it in a fundamental way. Since the political realm is all-embracing and affects all members of society, a just political order must strive to broaden not just the areas for the practice of democratic control but also the number of those who participate in matters pertaining to public life. The method of political consent seeks to provide members of society the power periodically to evaluate the performance of those who hold the political power in their name and for their sake. It is a mechanism of popular participation by which the community makes its leaders aware of their interests and needs. It is also a mechanism of participation that gives the community a sense of ownership and belonging. It seeks to provide "access to power of the exploited class"[4] while keeping power "at the service of the great popular majorities."[5]

From a liberation perspective, the legitimacy of political power and the authority of those who exercise it are very much dependent on their conscious effort to use it to empower the poor and marginal, to bring them into the political realm as beings of praxis. Power in this perspective is neither one-dimensional nor one-directional: it does not consist of making others act in agreement with our purposes. Rather, power is relational: it emerges and increases as we attempt to establish relationships of mutuality. Its distribution generates more power and a greater capacity to broaden the structures of justice for the well-being of all social members. Participatory self-government is a gauge by which to measure the process of liberation, particularly in its attempts to assist the poor in the process of overcoming their political passivity and marginality.

The quest for the concrete and effective participation of

the poor in political life makes the liberation concept of freedom and democracy distinct from the liberal notion of freedom and democracy that prevails in other Western industrial societies. In particular the quest distinguishes the liberation concept from the notion of *Democracia Restringida* that has predominated in North America's foreign policy toward Central and South America. As Gutiérrez has pointed out, this form of democracy amounts to nothing more than a formal restitution of a few freedoms and individual rights that leave intact the deep-rooted socioeconomic inequalities that presently exist.[6] It even allows the political left and other progressive sectors of society to enjoy political participation up to the point in which they become a viable alternative to the system. At this point, it does not hesitate to participate and justify even their brutal repression, all in the name of the preservation of Western Christian civilization. Ultimately, this form of democracy is nothing more than the means to incorporate sectors of the middle class into the present system and, in so doing, consolidate the power of the rich, now supported also by the middle class which benefits politically and economically from this arrangement.

Within poor nations, the need for economic development should not become an excuse to limit the participation of the people in the political process. This claim that economic development demands suspension of all political participation is generally an ideological device to justify the repression of the just claims of workers and peasants. One must come to terms with the fact that the scarcity poor Latin American nations experience has been the result of authoritarian governments, not of democratic regimes. Socialist societies are still plagued by this misconception.

Liberation theologians are not social contract theorists. Thus, for them, the method of consent is not part of an argument to justify the establishment of political society and the need for having a government. The state and its government are social givens and need no justification. It seems self-evident that social existence needs some form of government. The consent mechanism is merely a way of arguing for a particular form of government and the legitimate way it can use and exercise its power.

The mechanism of consent stresses the very important formal aspects of a democratic regime: the participation of all qualified adults in matters pertaining to the nomination and election of state officials; the opportunity and capacity to influence policy; the right to evaluate the performance of leaders; and the power to change the reign of government. In the language of rights, it has to do with the right to vote, to form political associations, to compete for political office, to choose between meaningful political alternatives, and the rights of free speech, association, press, and others that allow members of the political community to express their views publicly so that people can make informed choices.

From a liberation perspective, the formal dimensions of democracy are not as important as a more substantive view of democracy. The procedure of democracy must go hand in hand with the end result the process seeks. Thus, in the liberation perspective, an attempt is made to retrieve the original meaning of democracy as a class concept, that is, political rule by and for the poor which constitutes the true majority of society.

Democracy is understood as that sociopolitical order created by those who give preferential treatment to the poor and seek to use the resources and power of the state to attend to their needs for freedom and well-being. It refers not only to a kind of government but also to a particular way of ordering society. It has to do with the creation of an egalitarian society at both the economic and political level, together with the establishment of procedures that in fact enable the majority to prevail. It has to do with what Míguez Bonino calls the "ethos of human solidarity": "mankind as directed towards a form of life in which every member of society fully participates in all the possibilities afforded by nature and human relationships."[7] The procedural elements and the more substantive elements are intrinsically related and mutually reinforcing. The formal participation of the poor at all levels of political life determines whether or not the substantive goal of the majority gaining and receiving their freedom and well-being is going to be reached.

Liberation theologians are aware of how difficult it will be to establish democratic regimes within their nations. Some of these nations have had no democratic experience at all. Many external as well as internal barriers must be overcome. Externally, the struggle for the creation of a socialist democratic regime has to be carried out against Western democracies, in particular against the United States. The issue, of course, has to do with questions of economic interest and power. It also has to do with fundamentally different historical experiences and understandings of what democracy entails.

The liberal concept of democracy prevalent in most Western democracies, particularly in the United States, assumes that the sociopolitical and the socioeconomic realms are significantly different and autonomous from each other. It is within the political realm that it is meaningful for them to speak of broad popular participation and equality of rights. Their socioeconomic experience is one in which the majority of their citizens are integrated into the political and economic life of the nation. Their level of economic development allows them to create welfare programs for the marginalized, programs that are in many ways inadequate to the needs of those they serve but that still free them from the experience of extreme misery. This enables rich nations to speak in terms of having a "rough system of justice," one that can serve as a model for poor nations. In spite of the extreme inequalities that exist within rich nations themselves, they still claim that the democratic control of the political realm is possible and that it is in fact counterproductive to attempt to democratize the economic realm. As a result, there is suspicion and militant opposition against nations, in particular poor nations, that attempt to break this mold.

Liberation theologians question many of these assumptions on the basis of the sociohistorical and cultural differences that make it impossible for them to follow the liberal model. Given the extreme misery most of their people are subjected to, the fact that those integrated into the productive and political process are in fact the minority and that they cannot have a welfare system to attend the needs of the poor and marginal at the level of which the rich nations are capable, they argue that in their context it is impossible to speak of democracy at the political level without also having it at the economic level. In Gutiérrez's view, liberal democracy assumes an equality which is nonexistent.

The liberal concept of democracy has been an intrinsic part of the process of economic exploitation and political domination under which the rich nations of the West have subjected their poor counterparts. It still remains the ideology that justifies the interventionist policies of the United States that make it impossible for poor nations to obtain and consolidate their sovereignty.

The internal limitations within poor nations themselves are equally serious and costly to overcome. For the poor within poor nations, democracy is something still to be gained, requiring both the struggle to arrest political power and radically transform the social order. The poverty that is pervasive in their context does not allow for the market type democracy that exists in rich nations. The state simply cannot afford to become the supplier of the voters who use their votes, as money is used in the marketplace, to exchange for the goods and services they desire.

Within poor nations obtaining a democratic order depends on the possibility of enacting long-term and deep-rooted socioeconomic change as well as a new distribution of political power which is unlikely to come about by peaceful political means. We have argued for the virtues of the method of consent. Where there in fact exists rough political justice, the mechanism of consent seems to be normative. However, the method cannot apply in all political circumstances. Under conditions of social revolution it is not applicable.

From a liberation perspective, there is room to allow for the formation of a strong centralized political state, with all the dangers this entails, as a means and necessary step in the creation of conditions for democracy to emerge. However, even under the most unfavorable socioeconomic and political conditions, if democracy is to have any meaning at all, it cannot be a rule *for* the people but must also be rule *by* the people. The need for structural change and for a strong centralized state does not justify a violation of the people's right to participate at some level in the determination of their collective destiny. Avenues have to be created for the people to have access and input within the political decision-making process.

If, as is the case in most liberation struggles within poor nations, a one-party system takes the place of competing political parties, it is still equally important to have some mechanism of consent by which those at the bottom can participate in the selection of their leaders and be able to evaluate their policies. There must be some mechanism for the poor to let their leaders know their interest and expectations and for their leaders to explain the difficulties and nuances involved in reorganizing the social structure as a whole. People and their leaders must have some way of coming together to deliberate about alternative economic and political options.

Considerations about intraparty democracy are of special significance, given the strong nationalistic feeling and class solidarity that emerge after a revolutionary process becomes victorious. Immediately after a revolutionary process succeeds, the revolution must continue to fight and contain internal and external enemies. A time of crisis and a threat of civil war always exists; this makes it extremely difficult and unrealistic to have an open political process. Liberation movements tend thus to generate a contagious feeling of suspicion toward elements or groups that raise critical questions regarding the revolutionary process. They tend to silence not only the reactionary voices that seek to destabilize the process but also to silence the voices of people committed to the process but critical of its shortcomings. It is important that critical and prophetic voices be allowed a forum where they can be heard. It is important that there be a space for public debate and for the people to be able to make their leaders accountable. This is the only way people will be able to develop the political skills essential to their becoming beings of praxis and for the leaders to keep in touch with the base.

## Political Freedom

In a liberation perspective, persons as persons have a right to freedom. The right to freedom is the foundation and raison d'être of democracy. Democracy attempts to assure all the enjoyment of this freedom as well as maximize it for all.

Having a right to freedom implies that others and society as a whole are placed under the obligation not to unduly interfere with a person's actions and purposes. This even limits the way a person can treat him or herself. To surrender the right to freedom or to voluntarily decide to become a slave would be a violation of the right. One cannot, morally speaking, surrender what is intrinsic to our personhood. The right to freedom is intrinsic to our becoming beings of praxis.

Not to interfere, however, is not the only obligation we are placed under when it comes to the right to freedom. At times, we are placed under the obligation of providing goods and services that will enable a person to exercise freedom in the pursuit of her or his self-given purposes.

The right to freedom is exercised primarily within the political realm, through one's participation in the centers of decision making and through one's participation in social and political movements. However, freedom is not exhausted in the political realm. Other spheres call for self-initiation and creativity. Thus, a just political order seeks to preserve a sphere of privacy—a sphere not regulated by the state where persons can engage in creative activity. The creation and preservation of this space becomes even more urgent as the state's presence increases.

The liberation vision of the state is for a maximum state as opposed to the minimum state prevalent in the libertarian concept of justice. The maximum state is conceived as a welfare institution, the social institution that has the responsibility of providing for the freedom and well-being of all the citizens within society. It is the only social institution that has the necessary material resources to overcome the socioeconomic needs of the poor. It is the only one capable of initiating a radical social process to politicize all sectors of society. Fundamental social changes do not happen by accident, nor are they the product of the process that rules the market. They require a well-organized and popularly based and backed social will, which only the state can muster and direct.

The right to freedom is neither individualistic nor egoistic. It is not exhausted by doing whatever one wants as long as it does not hurt others. It also entails enabling others to experience freedom and have the capacity to give of themselves and carry out their life plans. Thus, although a person might not be directly responsible for another person's need or lack of freedom, if this person has what others need to significantly improve their condition and free themselves, she or he is obligated to help the neighbor. The sacrifice involved has to be kept within reasonable limits, but the smaller the sacrifice the more stringent the obligation.

No one has, as a matter of principle, the right to use all they own and produce. For the sake of sustaining and forwarding the common good, legitimate claims can be made against each person's resources. The right to freedom is a good, but it is not the only good—nor, in principle, even the highest good. It exists in tension with the right to well-being. These two rights are not perceived as antagonistic to each other, that is, obtaining one does not necessarily imply the negation of the other. On the contrary, many times the right to well-being enables people to have freedom since, as Míguez Bonino claims, " 'liberal freedoms' have little reality for economically, intellectually and even biologically submerged masses."[8] To free a person, for example, from economic need, fear of losing a job, racial and ethnic prejudice, ignorance, and lack of training, is in itself a significant step toward the realization of this person's freedom.

In principle, thus, neither of these rights has priority over the other. The question of their priority is to be established in the light of the prevailing sociohistorical circumstances. It is

reasonable, however, to claim that the right to well-being—
what one needs for the preservation of life—must be satisfied
first as a necessary condition for whatever life-plan or purpose
one seeks to realize. Still as sociocultural beings, humans need
both these rights to be satisfied; the right to the means necessary for the preservation of life must go hand in hand with the
freedom necessary to exercise our capacity to engage in purposeful action.

If freedom must be restricted to attend to the right to
well-being, it must be shown that this is necessary. Not just any
reason will do. One must be aware that the restriction of freedom usually goes hand in hand with nonattendance to the
needs of those who lose or are denied their capacity to express
and act publicly. At the same time one must also be aware that
those who tend to absolutize the right to freedom at all costs
tend to use it ideologically, that is, to deny the need for justice.
In Míguez Bonino's words, "When a person shouts 'liberty' in
Latin America today, one can immediately suspect him of being
a reactionary; and one is seldom wrong."[9] The decision to restrict freedom should not be made only by those in power. It
should have the consent of the community, and its restriction
should be short-term. The restriction of the right that enables
us to realize our potentialities and be able to make meaningful
choices cannot be taken lightly: our becoming beings of praxis
is at stake.

Freedom can be justly restricted when it is shown that the
short-term restriction will enable more members of the political community to enjoy this right. When it is restricted for the
sake of creating conditions that will enable the poor to overcome their marginality and political passivity, then its restriction can be justified.

We have seen that in general liberation theologians will
give priority to the right to well-being over the right to freedom
but not as a matter of principle. However, there are conditions
under which it seems they too would recognize that the right
to freedom might have priority. If the basic conditions of life
can be assured for all members of society, there would be very

few conditions that would justify the sacrifice of freedom for the sake of accumulating wealth. A just society does not need to strive for affluence but for that level of abundance that will enable its people to carry out their life-plans and live with dignity. The good life does not consist in never-ending consumption which will make scarcity chronic and impossible to solve.

After a given level of economic growth, one in which citizens can actualize meaningful life-plans, a just social order requires that all accumulation of wealth that demands a sacrifice of our freedom be forgone. Economic considerations become subordinate to political ones. The pleasures of establishing bonds of mutual support and common activity take precedence over the pleasures of individual consumption, doing takes precedence over having. It is possible to create a society in which all become actors. It is impossible to create a society in which all become insatiable consumers. It is in this context that Gutiérrez asserts that "the poor countries are not interested in modeling themselves after the rich countries. . . . poor countries are attempting to overcome material insufficiency and misery, but it is in order to achieve a more human society."[10]

## The Common Good

The term *common good* as a political category has had a longstanding tradition. The term has frequently been appealed to in religious social ethics. Roman Catholic social ethical thinking has always made reference to the common good. Presently the term is used less frequently. It is conceptually unclear and vague. What is that good that all are seen as holding in common?

Liberation theologians still find it useful to appeal to the common good but use it in ways that challenge the orthodox Roman Catholic interpretation as well as the classical liberal understanding. They argue that the term is related to the issue of social justice while recognizing that it cannot be simply identified with justice itself.

The traditional Roman Catholic concept of the common

good is a holistic one. Their understanding was based on a biological, organic model. They assumed an intrinsic affinity and interdependence between the good of the whole and the good of each part. The good of the whole was given priority over the good of the part. It was assumed that there existed a harmony between what is good for the whole and what is good for the part. It was expected that individuals agreed as to what the common good consisted of and recognized the need to adapt to the needs of society and to sacrifice for its well-being. This vision of the common good was much more viable within societies that were ethnically, racially, and culturally homogeneous. Within a pluralistic society its realization seems to imply the violation of our notions of human dignity and human rights.

Classical liberalism either denies that there is such a thing as the common good or has a mechanistic interpretation of it. The common good is seen as nothing more than the aggregate of the goods of the individuals that make up society. It reflects an instrumentalist understanding of social reality. Society is good only because within it exist the goods and services we need to satisfy our individual life-plans. In itself social life has little or no value. It is good thus only as an instrument for the realization of individual goals. There is no good for which the individual ought to sacrifice his or her interest and private notion of the good. In principle no sacrifice placed upon an individual can be justified in the name of the common good.

Liberation theologians argue that the content given to the common good cannot be defined once and for all. It is not a static state of affairs that can be achieved once and for all but rather must be defined and redefined in light of the concrete relationships that exist within a community. More than a given state of affairs, it is a historical venture, the creation of that social order in which the members of society are able to establish relationships that enable them to live with dignity so they can realize their potentialities.

From a liberation perspective, all meaningful considerations of the common good must assume the perspective and well-being of the poor. It must lead to the creation of relationships among the members of society such that no one achieves well-being from the exploitation and domination of another. It is only within the context of such social order that it makes sense to expect some to sacrifice dimensions of their self-interest for the well-being of the whole. Only those who see that ultimately society does in fact seek their well-being will refrain from obtaining certain benefits if these are seen as contributing to the preservation of just social relationships.

There is a good that we all must hold in common—the creation of social relationships, enabling us to become beings of praxis. But this good is not in principle harmonious. Individuals will always resist sacrificing their self-interest for the sake of the interest of the whole. What is good for the whole is not always good for all the parts—all the individuals who participate in relationship. Thus the quest and realization of the common good always implies making difficult choices in which some are called to sacrifice. It is still meaningful to speak of the common good as that social organization that intends to sustain the mutual well-being of all the members of society. Its preservation is seen as a social obligation and it is worthy not just of our individual contributions to it but also, when necessary, of some level of sacrifice. It is not meaningless to say that there are situations in which it is legitimate even to ask the poor to sacrifice some of their legitimate claims for the sake of preserving the social order that has proven itself to work for their liberation. Again, it is important to emphasize that the participation of the poor is essential in these matters. What cannot be compromised, what would make any notion of the common good meaningless, is to conceive it in terms that in principle exclude a sector of society from obtaining those goods and services necessary for the preservation of life.

# CONCLUSION

●

I have argued that to fully grasp what liberation theologians mean by justice, one must see it in relation to the three levels of meaning of the process of liberation: the socioeconomic level, the historico-utopian level, and the level of faith. The socioeconomic level makes us aware that issues of justice are primarily concerned with the reality of poverty as it manifests itself within a nation's particular sociohistorical coordinates. It awakens our suspicion toward those forms of thinking that engage in undue abstraction, mere logical consistency, and conceptual clarity that paralyze rather than encourage urgent and necessary action. It also makes us aware of the need to resist the ideological manipulation that empties social concepts of their power to motivate significant social commitment by converting them into tools that rationalize the exploitation and repression most Latin Americans are subjected to. Thus the goal of liberation theology is not love of humanity in general nor justice and human rights in the abstract, but rather, justice and human rights as they contribute to the liberation of the poor and their struggle for liberation within specific sociohistorical coordinates.

The level of faith, contrary to the opinions of some interpreters of this theological movement, is also essential to grasp what liberation theologians mean by justice because it is the underlying motivation for the commitment to a struggle that seems to be history's impossible possibility. Theology is not created to justify one's commitment to the process of liberation; rather it is the ultimate reason and basis for this commitment. It is at this level that all questions of meaning—including the meaning of justice—find their raison d'être. Theological reflection, the use of Christian symbols and language are not mere appendices added to socioeconomic analysis and concrete political options. They are in themselves necessary to grasp the fullness and depth of the human struggle for justice, of its historical becoming as well as the motivating force behind the political and moral options of those Christians that commit themselves to this struggle. It is at the level of faith that the commitment to justice assumes the character of a categorical imperative for the community of faith. We are not self-initiators of justice but merely respond to God's purpose for humanity. Our commitment to justice ultimately is based on grounds other than mere rationality. It is based on our abiding conviction that God desires and creates conditions for justice to emerge within our present historical circumstances. It is ultimately a biblical understanding of God as the God of justice and life that makes us commit ourselves to the struggle for liberation.

The level of faith defines and sustains the identity of the Christian commitment to justice. It provides the normative structure from which the community of faith can discriminate in its selection of the alternative concepts of justice provided by our cultural and political tradition. At the level of faith we also discover that the demands of justice can, and at times do, transcend what seems reasonable. Faith does call us at times to act beyond what reason can justify. Among the abiding convictions that inform the passion for justice of liberation theologians is the belief that God is creating conditions for a more just community to emerge precisely where there seem to be no subjective or objective conditions for community to emerge. A demand for justice, related to this conviction but difficult to defend on merely rational grounds, is the claim that having a need is in itself enough of a basis to make claims of justice against those who have the resources and abilities to satisfy them and that having the resources and abilities to satisfy the needs of others is enough of a basis to be placed under obligation to do so. Considerations of guilt and personal responsibility for the suffering of the needy become secondary.

From a liberation perspective our personal well-being is placed within the context of a larger whole or wholes we belong to. While the whole must provide for the realization of our potentialities and personal initiatives, it also has a right to place claims upon us and at times even demand that we sacrifice our self-interest for the sake of its preservation and well-being. Our life takes place and depends on a system of interrelationships whose health and preservation demand some measure of sacrifice of the individual members that participate within it. No justice can be had within the polis if some are not willing to sacrifice their privilege and well-being for the sake of enabling others to have an opportunity to realize their life. Without sacrifice social life would be impossible. What is important is that it be done with some consideration for justice.

Finally, at the level of faith we become aware of the limited and incomplete nature of our understanding and achievement of justice. We must take a firm stand on the basis of our convictions while recognizing that there are good reasons for alternative conceptions of justice to exist. We must keep in dialogue with these dissenting views because they can broaden and widen the scope of justice both theoretically and practically. Given the reality of pluralism, it is unlikely that a broad consensus on such practical matters will emerge. Still all attempts to come to agreement on certain fundamentals is worthwhile. It is, however, important to recognize that even in fundamentals there will be dissenting views. We must always be aware that no matter how much we seek to be for God's justice, our justice never fully conforms to God's.

Liberation theologians moved dialectically from the level of faith to the level of socioeconomic analysis and political options. This movement has been done without taking time to clarify the ethical elements that provide values and procedures that enable us to make more informed choices. Between the level of faith and the level of concrete political options there exists the level of value which is informed by the demands of concreteness of the political realm and the norms derived from the religious. At this level one must justify the options made regarding one's understanding of human nature, the good society, and one's concept of justice. I have argued that it is at this level that liberation theologians seem most unclear. However, I have attempted to show that this lack of clarity can be overcome since all the elements that are necessary to formulate a well-articulated notion of justice are present in their work.

From a liberation perspective, justice is based on the belief that every person as person is of equal worth and that their needs and claims must be given equal consideration. Our intrinsic worth as persons is not something we are entitled to on the basis of status, merit, social utility, birth, or desert. It is not something we can either win or lose by our actions; we cannot surrender it, nor can others give it to us. It is intrinsic to the kind of creatures we are.

We are social creatures in the strict sense of the word; that is, society is a good beyond and prior to considerations of the goods and services we can derive from it. We are who we are because of our social existence, because of those larger wholes that in many significant ways shape our personality. Thus, in our mutual dealings with others we are obliged to seek not only our good but to consider the good and interests of others. At times we are even obligated to surrender our interests so that others may fulfill theirs. This is what makes justice one of the principal virtues of social life, since it is mostly concerned with the needs and goods of the other, and it is to this end that it seeks to regulate the main institutions of social life.

Social justice is concerned mainly with the satisfaction of those needs that if left unfulfilled would harm a person in a fundamental way. It is imperative that all members of society have these needs fulfilled since their satisfaction is what enables persons to become beings of praxis. The end of the just society is to enable persons to become more, not just to have more. That is, it seeks to provide persons with goods and services they need so they can become responsible social actors and participate responsibly in the determination of their individual and collective destiny.

The criterion of need, although not the only relevant criterion of justice, does enjoy certain priority. It is conducive to the creation of an egalitarian society. Such a society seeks to make the basic equality all humans as human beings share visible at all levels of existence. It does not seek sameness but the erradication of all those forms of inequality that enable some to exploit and dominate others.

The basic needs all persons are entitled to are the right to economic well-being and political freedom. A just political community is one that seeks continuously to provide all members of society with these rights. All the members of society are entitled to what they need to live with dignity and to have a meaningful participation in those economic and political institutions that affect their lives in a fundamental way. On the basis of these rights, it is expected that communities will be formed within which persons are not only capable of recognizing an equal in the other but also have an inclination for caring for the well-being of others and for the community as a whole.

A just society is one in which its members recognize the need and obligation to support institutions whose business is to attend to the needs of those who have been left out. It is a society in which its members recognize that sacrifice is part of social existence and that the larger whole has a right over their resources and talents for the sake of preserving a just state of affairs that enables all members of society to enjoy a life worthy of the name human. From a liberation perspective the poor within society provide the standard to measure the justice of society and of those who live within it.

Internationally a similar principle of justice applies. Poor nations have a claim of justice over rich nations on the basis of their having needs which the rich nations have the ability and resources to fulfill. The capacity the rich nations have to enable poor nations to enjoy a higher level of economic well-being and exercise their freedom more, particularly within those international communities that affect their lives in a fundamental way, makes it a matter of obligation for them to serve those nations in spite of considerations of guilt and responsibility for the state of poverty of the poor nations.

Clearly, nations have first of all an obligation to their own citizens. This, however, is not the limit of their responsibility. As members of a global community, rich nations cannot remain indifferent to the needs of their global neighbors. The criterion of nationality, like those of race, sex, or ethnic origin, is not a relevant one for determining whose needs ought to be attended. A sign of the justice quality of a given nation is also revealed in its people's sensitivity and willingness to attend to the needs of strangers.

Given the national and international reality of extreme poverty, liberation theologians argue for the priority of the right to well-being over the right to freedom. The suppression of the right to freedom cannot be taken lightly and not just any condition can be used to justify it. Still there are legitimate reasons to limit it. For example, no one can be allowed to use personal talents and resources to dominate and exploit others. If for the sake of significantly improving the well-being of the poor there must be a limitation of the freedom of some members of society or of a social class, it is not unreasonable that their freedom be curtailed. When a decision must be made between allowing individuals to decide where they want to exercise their trade and allocating skilled personnel in areas where they are needed, the presumption is for the latter. The needs of the community in this case are given priority over the freedom of the individual to decide where he or she will exercise her or his trade. This is perceived as a way of increasing the possibility for more members of society to be able to enjoy the right to freedom. If liberation theologians establish a priority between the right to freedom and the right to well-being, it is clear that they recognize that both are indispensable for persons to become beings of praxis. Both constitute the basic needs people must have satisfied if they are to realize their potential as historical agents.

Liberation theologians argue that in their context only some form of socialism will create objective and subjective conditions to break or significantly minimize their condition of dependence and open the possibility for the creation of a society that seeks to attend to the needs of all its members. The present capitalist system and the social groups that advocate it have proven to be incapable of moving in this direction. Only the poor themselves will provide the efficient cause and vision for a new historic project that seeks to be life-giving and life-sustaining for all members of society.

# NOTES
•

## Chapter 1:
## The Centrality of Justice in Latin American
## Theology of Liberation

1. José Míguez Bonino, *Doing Theology in a Revolutionary Situation*, (Philadelphia: Fortress, 1975), 62.
2. Gustavo Gutiérrez, "The Voice of the Poor in the Church," *Proceedings of the Catholic Theological Society of America* 33 (1978): 30–31.
3. Gutiérrez, *The Power of the Poor in History*, trans. Robert R. Barr (Maryknoll, N.Y.: Orbis Books, 1983), 101–102. Originally published as *La fuerza histórica de los pobres* (Peru: Centro de Estudios y Publicaciones, 1979).
4. Hugo Assmann, *Teología desde la praxis de la liberación*, (Salamanca: Ediciones Sígueme, 1973), 65. All translations of titles cited in Spanish are those of the author.
5. José Míguez Bonino, "Historical Praxis and Christian Identity," in *Frontiers of Theology in Latin America*, ed. Rosino Gibellini, trans. John Drury (Maryknoll, N.Y.: Orbis, 1979), 280.
6. Míguez Bonino, *Doing Theology*, 149.
7. José Porfirio Miranda, *Being and the Messiah: The Message of St. John*, trans. John Eagleson (Maryknoll, N.Y.: Orbis, 1977), 73–74.
8. Míguez Bonino, *Doing Theology*, 128, 29.
9. Gustavo Gutiérrez, *A Theology of Liberation: History, Politics and Salvation*, trans. Sister Caridad Inda and John Eagleson (Maryknoll, N.Y.: Orbis, 1973), 149.
10. Gutiérrez, *The Power of the Poor*, 200–201.
11. Gutiérrez, *La fuerza histórica de los pobres*, 393; *The Power of the Poor*, 214.
12. Assmann, *Teología desde la praxis*, 133.
13. Gustavo Gutiérrez and Richard Shaull, *Liberation and Change*, ed. Ronald Stone (Atlanta: John Knox, 1977), 31.
14. José Míguez Bonino, "Religious Commitment and Human Rights: A Christian Perspective" (Dublin, 1978), 6, mimeographed.
15. Míguez Bonino, "Religious Commitment and Human Rights," 7–8.

16. Ibid., 11.
17. Ibid., 12.
18. Ibid., 13.
19. Ibid., 14–15.
20. Gutiérrez, *The Power of the Poor,* 211–12. Cf. José Porfirio Miranda, *Marx and the Bible: A Critique of the Philosophy of Oppression,* trans. John Eagleson (Maryknoll, N.Y.: Orbis, 1974), 93.
21. Miranda, *Being and the Messiah,* 36, 37.
22. Gutiérrez, *A Theology of Liberation,* 237.
23. Miranda, *Marx and the Bible,* 87.

Chapter 2:
Liberation and Justice

1. Gutiérrez, *A Theology of Liberation,* 81.
2. Ibid., 174.
3. Hugo Assmann, *Theology for a Nomad Church,* trans. Paul Burns, intro. Frederick Herzog (Maryknoll, N.Y.: Orbis, 1976), 129–30.
4. Walt Whitman Rostow, *The Stages of Economic Growth: A Non-Communist Manifesto* (Cambridge: Cambridge University Press, 1962), 4, 6, 7.
5. Gino Germani, "De la sociedad a la participación total en América Latina," in *América Latina: Ensayos de interpretación sociológico-político,* ed. Fernando H. Cardoso and Francisco Weffort (Chile: Editorial Universitaria, 1970), 220.
6. Raul Prebisch, *Nueva political comercial para el desarrollo* (Mexico: Fondo de Cultura Económica, 1964), 203–219. Cf. Werner Baer, "The Economics of Prebisch and ECLA," in Charles T. Nisbet, *Latin America: Problems in Economic Development* (New York: The Free Press, 1969), 203–219.
7. Helio Jaguaribe, *Political Development: A General Theory and a Latin American Case Study* (New York: Harper & Row, 1973). Cf. Helio Jaguaribe, "Dependencia y autonomia en América Latina," in *La dependencia politico-economica de America Latina,* by Helio Jaguaribe, et al. (Mexico: Siglo Veintiuno, 1977).
8. Fernando H. Cardoso and Enzo Falleto, "Dependencia y desarrollo en América Latina," in *Aspectos sociológicos del desarrollo en América Latina,* ed. by Centro Intercultural de Documentación (Mexico: CIDOC, no. 17, 1968), 33.
9. Theotonio dos Santos, "The Structure of Dependence," *American Economic Review* 60(May 1970):232.
10. Aníbal Quijano, "Dependencia, cambio social y urbanización en Latinomerica," in *América Latina: Ensayos de interpretación*

*socio-política,* ed. Fernando H. Cardoso and Francisco Weffort (Chile: Editorial Universitaria, 1970), 99.

11. Theotonio dos Santos, *Fascismo o socialismo: El neuvo carácter de la dependencia y el dilema lationamericano* (Argentina: Ediciones Periferia, 1973), 69.

12. Rudolfo Stavenhagen, "Seven Fallacies about Latin America," in *Latin America, Reform or Revolution?* ed. James Petras and Maurice Zeitlin (Greenwich, Conn.: Fawcett, 1968), 20.

13. Paulo Freire, *Cultural Action for Freedom* (Cambridge, Mass.: Harvard Educational Review, 1970), 34.

14. Jaguaribe, *Political Development,* 418.

15. Dos Santos, *Fascismo o socialismo,* 43.

16. Míguez Bonino, *Doing Theology,* 6–7.

17. José Míguez Bonino, "How Does United States Presence Help, Hinder or Compromise Christian Mission in Latin America?" *Review and Expositor* 74(Spring 1977): 177–78.

18. Ibid., 179–80.

19. Míguez Bonino, *Doing Theology,* 18; cf., 32–33.

20. James M. Gustafson, *Can Ethics Be Christian?* (Chicago: University of Chicago Press, 1975), 94–99.

21. José Míguez Bonino, *Christians and Marxists: The Mutual Challenge to Revolution* (Grand Rapids, Mich.: William B. Eerdmans, 1976), 101–2.

22. Miranda, *Marx and the Bible,* 7, 11.

23. Míguez Bonino, *Doing Theology,* 31.

24. Ibid., 126–27.

25. Assmann, *Teología desde la praxis,* 204.

26. Míguez Bonino, *Doing Theology,* 128.

27. Míguez Bonino, *Christians and Marxists,* 7–8.

28. Gustavo Gutiérrez, "Contestation in Latin America," in *Contestation in the Church,* ed. Teodoro Jiménez Urresti, trans. Paul Burns, Concilium 68 (New York: Herder and Herder, 1971), 50.

29. Gutiérrez, *Theology of Liberation,* 187 n. 93, 174.

30. Assmann, *Teología desde la praxis,* 162.

31. Gutiérrez, *Theology of Liberation,* 295, 159.

32. Ibid., x.

33. Míguez Bonino, *Christians and Marxists,* 130. See also Gutiérrez, *Theology of Liberation,* 237; Miranda, *Being and the Messiah,* 29.

34. Gutiérrez, *Theology of Liberation,* 146. See also Míguez Bonino, *Doing Theology,* 40; Assmann, *Teología desde la praxis,* 133–34.

35. Assmann, *Teología desde la praxis,* 134.

36. Míguez Bonino, *Doing Theology,* 40.

37. Míguez Bonino, *Christians and Marxists,* 92.

38. Assmann, *Teología desde la praxis*, 136.
39. Hugo Assmann, "El tercer mundo comienza a crear un lenguaje alternativo sobre los derechos humanos," in *Carter y la lógica del imperialismo* (Costa Rica: EDUCA, 1978), 455.
40. Assmann, *Teología desde la praxis*, 295.
41. Gutiérrez, *Theology of Liberation*, 36, quoting Dietrich Bonhoeffer, *Creation and Fall, Temptation* (New York: The Macmillan Company, 1966), 37.
42. Gutiérrez, *Theology of Liberation*, 112, quoting "El Presente de Chile y el Evangelio" (Santiago de Chile, 1970), mimeographed.
43. Gutiérrez, *Theology of Liberation*, 137–38.
44. Ibid., 168.
45. Ibid., 175–76.
46. Ibid., 175, cf., 35.
47. Míguez Bonino, *Christians and Marxists*, 129.
48. Míguez Bonino, *Doing Theology*, 111.
49. Gutiérrez, *Theology of Liberation*, 35.
50. Miranda, *Marx and the Bible*, 168.
51. Míguez Bonino, *Doing Theology*, xxv.
52. José Míguez Bonino, "Teología y liberación," in *ISAL* 3(1970):2.
53. Gustavo Gutiérrez, "Revelation and the Proclamation of God in History," in *Jesuit Project for Third World Awareness* (Chicago, n.d.), 7, mimeographed. See also Míguez Bonino, *Christians and Marxists*, 35, 67–68, 107.
54. Gutiérrez, "Revelation and the Proclamation of God," Ibid., 11–12. See also Míguez Bonino, *Christians and Marxists*, 38.
55. Miranda, *Marx and the Bible*, 136.
56. Assmann, *Teología desde la praxis*, 156, 226.
57. Míguez Bonino, *Christians and Marxists*, 109–110. See also *Doing Theology*, 166.
58. Míguez Bonino, *Christians and Marxists*, 104.
59. Miranda, *Marx and the Bible*, 61.
60. Assmann, *Teología desde la praxis*, 135.
61. Míguez Bonino, *Doing Theology*, 114.
62. Miranda, *Marx and the Bible*, 62, quoting Pierre Bigo, *La doctrine sociale de l'Eglise* (Paris: Presses Universitaires de France, 1965), 378.
63. Míguez Bonino, *Doing Theology*, 114, quoting Paul Ricoeur, "El conflicto signo de contra diccion y de unidad?" *Criterio* no. 1668 (Buenos Aires, 24 May 1973): 255.
64. Assmann, *Teología desde la praxis*, 117.
65. Gutiérrez, *Theology of Liberation*, 202.
66. Míguez Bonino, *Ama y haz lo que quieras* (Buenos Aires: Editorial Escatón, 1976), 61.

67. Míguez Bonino, *Christians and Marxists*, 138.
68. Assmann, *Teología desde la praxis*, 148–49.
69. Míguez Bonino, *Christians and Marxists*, 112.
70. Jon Sobrino, *The True Church and the Poor*, trans. Matthew J. O'Connel (Maryknoll, N.Y.: Orbis Books, 1984), 39–63.
71. Gutiérrez, *Theology of Liberation*, 71.
72. Miranda, *Marx and the Bible*, 227.
73. Gutiérrez, *Theology of Liberation*, 269.
74. Míguez Bonino, *Doing Theology*, 167, 169.
75. Hugo Assmann, et al., *Cristianos por el socialismo: Exigencia de una opció* (Montevideo, Uruguay: Tierra Nueva, 1973), 156–157.
76. Gustavo Gutiérrez, "Liberation, Theology and Proclamation," in *The Mystical and Political Dimension of the Christian Faith*, ed. Claude Geffre and Gustavo Gutiérrez, Concilium 96 (New York: Herder and Herder, 1974), 64. See also Gutiérrez, "Contestation in Latin America," 50, and Míguez Bonino, *Doing Theology*, 111–12.
77. Assmann, *Teología desde la praxis*, 90–91.
78. Míguez Bonino, *Christians and Marxists*, 140.
79. Ibid., 138.
80. Ibid., 129–30.

Chapter 3:
Liberation Justice and Alternative Concepts of Justice in the Western World

1. Among the authors considered in this section are Thomas Aquinas, *Summa Theologica*, trans. Fathers of the English Dominican Province, rev. Daniel J. Sullivan, 2 vols. (Chicago: Encyclopaedia Britannica, 1952), and "Summa Contra Gentiles," in *Aquinas, Selected Political Writings*, ed. A. Passerin d'Entrèves, trans. J. G. Dawson (Oxford: Basil Blackwell and Mott, 1970); Jacques Maritain, *Neuf Leçons sur les notions premiéres de la philosophie morale* (Paris: Pierre Téqui, 1951), and *Man and the State* (Chicago: University of Chicago, 1951); and A. Passerin d'Entrèves, *The Natural Law: An Introduction to Legal Philosophy* (London: Hutchinson University Library, 1970).
2. David Miller, *Social Justice* (Oxford: Clarendon, 1976), 285:

> . . . in feudal society the occupants of different roles were linked to one another by ties of personal dependence. Relationships of this type naturally created a sense of mutual obligation rather than a sense of mutual indifference. Although there was no question of the lord acknowledging the serf as his equal, he did recognize that they were con-

nected by a personal bond, and that he therefore had responsibility for the serf's welfare. . . . This is the basis of the recognition given to the claims of need in the feudal conception of justice. A condition of need gave a man a just claim on the resources of those placed in privileged positions, and especially of course on the master to whom he was personally tied.

3. Jacques Maritain, *Integral Humanism: Temporal and Spiritual Problems of a New Christendom,* trans. Joseph W. Evans (London: Notre Dame Press, 1973).

4. Míguez Bonino, *Doing Theology,* 115; see also *Christians and Marxists,* 114.

5. Miranda, *Being and the Messiah,* 78. See also Assmann, *Theology of a Nomad Church,* 76–77.

6. For a brief analysis of the development of the Christian Democratic party in Chile see Juan Luis Segundo, *The Liberation of Theology,* trans. John Drury (Maryknoll, N.Y.: Orbis, 1976), 90–95, and Míguez Bonino, *Christians and Marxists,* 21–23.

7. Among the authors considered in this section are Hans Kelsen, "The Pure Theory of Law," in *The Nature of Law: Readings in Legal Philosophy,* ed. M. P. Golding (New York: Random House, 1966); John Austin, "Law as the Sovereign's Command," in Ibid.; Alf Ross, "Directives and the 'Validity' of Law," in Ibid.; and Dennis Lloyd, *The Idea of Law* (Baltimore: Penguin Books, 1976).

8. Golding, *The Nature of Law,* 126.

9. Miranda, *Being and the Messiah,* 30.

10. Ibid., ix, 29–30.

11. Míguez Bonino, *Ama y haz lo que quieras,* 41–43, author's translation.

12. Miranda, *Marx and the Bible,* 168.

13. Ibid., 146, 158.

14. Among the authors considered in this section are Ronald Dworkin, *Taking Rights Seriously* (Cambridge, Mass.: Harvard University Press, 1977); Jacques Maritain, *Challenges and Renewal: Selected Readings,* ed. Joseph W. Evans and Leo R. Ward (New York: Meridian Books, 1966); David Miller, *Social Justice;* and A. Passerin d'Entrèves, *The Natural Law: An Introduction to Legal Philosophy.*

15. Dworkin, *Taking Rights Seriously,* 176, 177.

16. Passerin d'Entrèves, *The Natural Law,* 55.

17. Ibid., 60.

18. Miller, *Social Justice,* 309.

19. Gutiérrez and Shaull, *Liberation and Change,* 71.

20. Miranda, *Marx and the Bible,* 19.

## Chapter 4:
### Economic Justice

1. Gutiérrez, *La fuerza histórica*, 209.
2. Míguez Bonino, *Doing Theology*, 119. See also Miranda, *Marx and the Bible*, 5–6.
3. José Porfirio Miranda, *Hambre y sed de justicia* (Mexico: n.p., 1972), 46–47. See also Míguez Bonino, *Ama y haz lo que quieras*, 98.
4. Hugo Assmann, "Technología y poder en la perspectiva de la teología de la liberación," in *Estudios Ecuménicos* (Mexico: La Iglesia y los derechos humanos) 37 (1979), 29–30.
5. Miranda, *Marx and the Bible*, 1–2.
6. Miranda, *Hambre y sed de justicia*, 46–47.
7. Ibid., 44.
8. Ibid., 45.
9. Ibid., 50.
10. Hugo Assmann, "Breves consideraciones al margen del informe final del encuentro de Oaxtepec," *Estudios Ecuménicos* 38 (1979).
11. Miranda, *Hambre y sed de justicia*, 44–45.
12. Denis Goulet, *The Cruel Choice: A New Concept in the Theory of Development* (New York: Atheneum, 1971), 143.

## Chapter 5:
### Political Justice

1. Assmann, *Teología desde la praxis*, 141.
2. Gutiérrez, *The Power of the Poor*, 38.
3. Míguez Bonino, *Christians and Marxists*, 123.
4. Gutiérrez, *Theology of Liberation*, 26.
5. Gutiérrez and Shaull, *Liberation and Change*, 77.
6. Gutiérrez, *La fuerza histórica*, 339, *The Power of the Poor*, 187.
7. Míguez Bonino, *Christians and Marxists*, 119.
8. Ibid., 88. See also *Doing Theology*, 16.
9. Ibid., 17.
10. Gutiérrez, *Theology of Liberation*, 22.

# BIBLIOGRAPHY

•

Aguilar, Alonso. *Pan Americanism: From Monroe to the Present.* Translated by Asa Zatz. New York: Monthly Review Press, 1968.

Alves, Rubem A. *A Theology of Human Hope.* Foreword by Harvey Cox. New York: World Publishing Co., 1969; reprint ed., St. Meinrad, Ind.: Abbey Press, 1975.

――――. "Theology and the Liberation of Man." In *In Search of a Theology of Development,* edited by Sodepax. Switzerland: Sodepax, 1969. Pp. 75–92.

――――. *Tomorrow's Child: Imagination, Creativity and the Rebirth of Culture.* New York: Harper and Row, 1972.

Andreski, Stanislav. *Parasitism and Subversion: The Case of Latin America.* New York: Schocken Books, 1969.

*Aquinas: Selected Political Writings.* Edited by A. P. d'Entrèves. Translated by J. G. Dawson. Oxford: Basil Blackwell and Mott, Ltd., 1970.

Aquinas, Thomas. "Summa Contra Gentiles." In *Aquinas: Selected Political Writings.* Edited by A. P. D'Entrèves. Translated by J. G. Dawson. Oxford: Basil Blackwell and Mott, Ltd., 1970.

――――. *The Summa Theologica.* Translated by Fathers of the English Dominican Province. Revised by Daniel J. Sullivan. 2 vols. Chicago: Encyclopaedia Britannica, Inc., 1952.

Assmann, Hugo. "Breves consideraciones al margen del informe final del encuentro de Oaxtepec." *Estudios Ecuménicos* 38 (1979): 50–53.

Assmann, Hugo. "El tercer mundo comienza a crear un lenguaje alternativo sobre los derechos humanos." In *Carter y la lógica del imperialismo.* 2 vols. Edited by Hugo Assmann. Costa Rica: EDUCA, 1978. Pp. 451–56.

――――. "La tarea común de las ciencias sociales y de la teología en el desenmascaramiento de la necrofilia del capitalismo." In *Capitalismo: Violencia y anti-vida. La opresión de las mayorías y la domesticación de los dioses.* Vol. 1. Edited by Elsa Tamez and Saúl Trinidad. Costa Rica: EDUCA, 1978. Pp. 21–37.

――――. "Tecnología y poder en la perspectiva de la teología de la liberación." *Estudios Ecuménicos* 37 (1979): 27–36.

204     Justice in Latin American Theology of Liberation

——. *Teología desde la praxis de la liberación*. Salamanca: Ediciones Sígueme, 1973.

——. "The Power of Christ in History: Conflicting Christologies and Discernment." In *Frontiers of Theology in Latin America*. Edited by Rosino Gibellini. Translated by John Drury. New York: Orbis Books, 1979. Pp. 133–50.

——. *Theology for a Nomad Church*. Translated by Paul Burns. Introduction by Frederick Herzog. Maryknoll, N.Y.: Orbis Books, 1976.

——, ed. *Carter y la lógica del imperialismo*, 2 vols. Costa Rica: EDUCA, 1978.

Assmann, Hugo; Bach, Luis; Blanes, José; Míguez Bonino, José; Girardi, J.; and Coste, R. *Cristianos por el socialismo: Exigencia de una opción*. Montevideo, Uruguay: Tierra Nueva, 1973.

Austin, John. "Law as the Sovereign's Command." In *The Nature of Law: Readings in Legal Philosophy*. Edited by M. P. Golding. New York: Random House, 1966. Pp. 77–98.

Barr, Werner. "The Economics of Prebisch and ECLA." In *Latin America: Problems of Economic Development*. Edited by Charles T. Nisbet. New York: The Free Press, 1969. Pp. 203–19.

Bird, Otto A. *The Idea of Justice*. New York: Frederich A. Praeger, 1967.

Booth, A. John, and Seligson, Mitchell A., eds. *Political Participation in Latin America*. 2 vols. New York: Holmes and Meier Publishers, 1978–79.

Cahn, Edmond. *A Sense of Injustice*. Bloomington: Indiana University Press, 1964.

Cámara, Helder P. "Human Rights and the Liberation of Man in the Americas: Reflections and Responses." In *Human Rights and the Liberation of Man in the Americas*. Edited by Louis M. Colonnese. Notre Dame: University of Notre Dame Press, 1970. Pp. 259–68.

Cardoso, Fernando H. *Ideologías de la burguesía industrial en sociedades dependientes (Argentina y Brasil)*. México: Siglo Veintiuno Editores, S.A., 1974.

Cardoso, Fernando H., and Faletto, Enzo. "Dependencia y desarrollo en América Latina." In *Aspectos sociológicos del desarrollo en América Latina*. Edited by Centro Intercultural de Documentación. México: CIDOC No. 17, 1968. Pp. 1–41.

——. *Dependencia y desarrollo en América Latina: Ensayo de interpretación sociológica*. México:SigloVeintiunoEditores,S.A.,1976.

——. "Los agentes sociales de cambio y conservación." In *Aspectos sociológicos del desarrollo en América Latina*. Edited by Centro Intercultural de Documentación. México: CIDOC No. 17, 1968. Pp. 8/1–27.

Cardoso, Fernando H., and Weffort, Francisco. *América Latina: Ensayos de interpretación sociológico-política.* Chile: Editorial Universitaria, S.A., 1970.

Centro de Estudios y Publicaciones, ed. *Signos de liberación: Testimonios de la Iglesia en América Latina, 1969–1973.* Lima: Centro de Estudios y Publicaciones, 1973.

Cockcroft, James D.; Frank, André Gunder; and Johnson, Dale L. *Dependence and Underdevelopment: Latin America's Political Economy.* New York: Anchor Books, 1972.

Passerin d'Entrèves, Alessandro. *Natural Law: An Introduction to Legal Philosophy.* London: Hutchinson University Library, 1970.

Dos Santos, Theotonio. *Contradicciones del imperialismo contemporáneo.* Venezuela: Editorial la Enseñanza Viva, 1973.

———. *Dependencia y cambio social.* Chile: Centro de Estudios Socio-Económicos (CESO), 1970.

———. "El capitalismo colonial según André Gunder Frank," *Monthly Review* (November 1968): 139–50.

———. *Socialismo o fascismo: El nuevo carácter de la dependencia y el dilema latinoamericano.* Buenos Aires: Ediciones Periferia S.R.L., 1973.

Dos Santos, Theotonio. "The Structure of Dependence." *The American Economic Review* 60 (May 1970): 231–36.

Dussel, Enrique. *Historia de la Iglesia en América Latina.* Barcelona: Editorial Nova Terra, 1972.

Dworkin, Ronald. *Taking Rights Seriously.* Massachusetts: Harvard University Press, 1977.

Feinberg, Joel. *Rights, Justice, and the Bounds of Liberty.* New Jersey: Princeton University Press, 1980.

Fierro, Alfredo. *The Militant Gospel: A Critical Introduction to Political Theologies.* Translated by John Drury. Maryknoll, N.Y.: Orbis Books, 1977.

Fiorenza, Francis Schussler. "Political Theology as Foundational Theology." In *Proceedings of the Catholic Theological Society of America* 32 (1977): 142–77.

Frank, André Gunder. *Capitalism and Underdevelopment in Latin America: Historical Studies of Chile and Brazil.* New York: Monthly Review Press, 1969.

———. *Latin America: Underdevelopment or Revolution.* New York: Monthly Review Press, 1970.

———. *Lumpenbourgeoisie: Lumpendevelopment.* New York: Monthly Review Press, 1972.

Frankena, William. "The Concept of Social Justice." In *Social Justice.* Edited by Richard Brandt. Englewood Cliffs, N.J.: Prentice-Hall, 1962. Pp. 1–29.

Freire, Paulo. *Cultural Action for Freedom.* Monograph Series No. 1.

Massachusetts: Harvard Educational Review and Center for the Study of Development and Social Change, 1970.

——. "Letter to a Young Theologian." In Assmann, Hugo, *Teología desde la praxis de la liberación.* Salamanca: Ediciones Sígueme, 1973. P. 62.

——. *Pedagogy of the Oppressed.* Translated by Myra Bergman Ramos. New York: Herder and Herder, 1970.

Friedman, Milton. "Foreign Economic Aid: Means and Objectives." *The Yale Review* 47 (1957–58): 500–16.

Gewirth, Alan. "Political Justice." In *Social Justice.* Edited by Richard Brandt. Englewood Cliffs, N.J.: Prentice-Hall, 1962. Pp. 119–169.

Gewirth, Alan. *Reason and Morality.* Chicago: University of Chicago Press, 1978.

Ginsberg, Morris. *On Justice in Society.* Baltimore: Penguin Books, 1965.

Golding, M. P., ed. *The Nature of Law: Readings in Legal Philosophy.* New York: Random House, 1966.

González Casanova, Pablo. *La democracia en México.* México: Ediciones ERA, S.A., 1967.

——. *Sociología de la explotación.* México: Siglo Veintiuno Editores S.A., 1975.

Goulet, Denis. *The Cruel Choice: A New Concept in the Theory of Development.* New York: Atheneum, 1973.

Gustafson, James M. *Can Ethics Be Christian?* Chicago: The University of Chicago Press, 1975.

——. "Contestation in Latin America." In *Contestation in the Church.* Translated by Paul Burns. Edited by Teodoro Jiménez Urresti. Concilium 68. New York: Herder and Herder, 1971. Pp. 40–52.

——. *Cristianismo y Tercer Mundo.* Colección "Pueblo de Dios," Serie D., Num. 10. Bilbao: Edita Zero, 1973.

——. "Faith as Freedom: Solidarity with the Alienated and Confidence in the Future." *Horizons* 2 (Spring 1975): 25–60.

——. *La fuerza histórica de los pobres.* Perú: Centro de Estudios y Publicaciones, 1979.

Gutiérrez, Gustavo. "A Latin American Perception of a Theology of Liberation." In *Conscientization for Liberation.* Edited by Louis M. Colonnese. Washington, D.C.: Division for Latin America United States Catholic Conference, 1971. Pp. 57–80.

——. "Liberation Movements and Theology." Translated by J. P. Donnelly. In *Jesus Christ and Human Freedom.* Edited by E. Schillebeeckx and Bas van Iersel. Concilium 93. New York: Herder and Herder, 1974. Pp. 135–46.

——. "Liberation Praxis and Christian Faith." Translated by John

Drury. In *Frontiers of Theology in Latin America.* Edited with a preface by Rosino Gibellini. Maryknoll, N.Y.: Orbis Books, 1979. Pp. 1–33.

Gutiérrez, Gustavo. "Liberation, Theology and Proclamation." In *The Mystical and Political Dimension of the Christian Faith.* Concilium 96. Edited by Claude Geffré and Gustavo Gutiérrez. New York: Herder and Herder, 1974. Pp. 57–77.

———. "Notes for a Theology of Liberation." *Theological Studies* 31 (June 1970): 243–61.

———. "The Poor in the Church." Translated by Dinah Livingstone. In *The Poor and the Church.* Edited by Norbert Greinacher and Alois Müller. Concilium 104. New York: Seabury Press, 1977. Pp. 11–16.

———. *The Power of the Poor in History.* Translated by Robert R. Barr. Maryknoll, N.Y.: Orbis Books, 1983.

———. "Praxis de liberación y fe cristiana." In *Signos de liberación: Testimonios de la Iglesia en la América Latina 1969–1973.* Lima: Centro de Estudios y Publicaciones, 1973. Pp. 13–36.

———. "Revelation and the Proclamation of God in History." In *Jesuit Project for Third World Awareness.* Chicago, n.d. (Mimeographed).

———. *Teología de la liberación: Perspectivas.* Lima: Centro de Estudios y Publicaciones, 1971.

———. "Teología desde el reverso de la historia." In *La fuerza histórica de los pobres.* Perú: Centro de Estudios y Publicaciones, 1979. Pp. 303–394.

———. *A Theology of Liberation: History, Politics and Salvation.* Translated and edited by Sister Caridad Inda and John Eagleson. Maryknoll, N.Y.: Orbis Books, 1973.

———. "The Voice of the Poor in the Church." In *Proceedings of the Catholic Theological Society of America* 33: 30–34.

———. *We Drink from Our Own Wells: The Spiritual Journey of a People.* Translated by Matthew J. O'Connell. Maryknoll, N.Y.: Orbis Books, 1984.

Gutiérrez, Gustavo, and Shaull, Richard. *Liberation and Change.* Edited with an introduction by Ronald H. Stone. Atlanta: John Knox Press, 1977.

Hirschman, Albert O., ed. *Latin American Issues: Essays and Comments.* New York: The Twentieth Century Fund, 1961.

Honore, A. M. "Social Justice." In *Essays in Legal Philosophy.* Edited by Robert S. Summers. California: University of California Press, 1968. Pp. 61–94.

Hoselitz, Berthold F. *Sociological Factors in Economic Development.* Glencoe: The Free Press, 1960.

208     Justice in Latin American Theology of Liberation

Jaguaribe, Helio. *Political Development: A General Theory and a Latin American Case Study.* New York: Harper and Row, 1973.
Jaguaribe, Helio; Ferrer, Aldo; Wionczek, Miguel S.; and Dos Santos, Theotonio. *La dependencia político-económica de América Latina.* México: Siglo Veintiuno Editores, S.A., 1977.
Kelsen, Hans. "The Pure Theory of Law." In *The Nature of Law: Readings in Legal Philosophy.* Edited by M. P. Golding. New York: Random House, 1966. Pp. 108–34.
Latin American Episcopal Council. *The Church in the Present-Day Transformation of Latin America in the Light of the Council.* 2 vols. Bogota: General Secretariat of CELAM, 1970.
Lloyd, Dennis. *The Idea of law.* Baltimore: Penguin Books, 1976.
Lopes, José Leite. *La ciência y el dilema de América Latina: Dependencia o liberación.* Translated by Mónica Peralta Ramos. Buenos Aires: Siglo Veintiuno Argentina Editores, S.A., 1972.
McClelland, David. *The Achieving Society.* Princeton: Van Nostrand, 1961.
Maritain, Jacques. *Challenges and Renewal.* Selected Readings. Edited by Joseph W. Evans and Leo R. Ward. New York: Meridian Books, 1966.
————. *Integral Humanism: Temporal and Spiritual Problems of a New Christendom.* Translated by Joseph W. Evans. London: Notre Dame Press, 1973.
————. *Man and the State.* Chicago: University of Chicago Press, 1951.
————. *Neuf leçons sur les notions premiéres de la philosophie morale.* Paris: Pierre Téqui, 1951.
Míguez Bonino, José. *Ama y haz lo que quieras: Una ética para el hombre nuevo.* Buenos Aires: Editorial Escatón, 1976.
————. *Christians and Marxists: The Mutual Challenge to Revolution.* Grand Rapids, Mich.: William B. Eerdmans Publishing Co., 1976.
————. *Doing Theology in a Revolutionary Situation.* Philadelphia: Fortress Press, 1975.
————. "Ecclesia Pauper-Ecclesia Pauperum en el Vaticano II y en la teología católica latinoamericana reciente." In *Los pobres: Encuentro y compromiso.* Edited by I.S.E.D.E.T. Buenos Aires: Editorial La Aurora, 1978. Pp. 133–47.
————. "Historical Praxis and Christian Identity." In *Frontiers of Theology in Latin America.* Edited by Rosino Gibellini. Translated by John Drury. New York: Orbis Books, 1979. Pp. 260–83.
————. "How Does United States Presence Help, Hinder or Compromise Christian Mission in Latin America." *Review and Expositor* 74 (Spring 1977): 173–82.
Míguez Bonino, José. "Los derechos humanos, ¿de quiénes?" In *Carter y la lógica del imperialismo.* Vol. 2. Edited by Hugo Assmann. Costa Rica: EDUCA, 1978. Pp. 333–38.

―――. "Nuevas perspectívas teologicas." In *Pueblo oprimido, señor de la historia.* Edited by Iglesia y Sociedad. Montevideo: Tierra Nueva, 1972. Pp. 197–212.

―――. "Religious Commitment and Human Rights: A Christian Perspective." Dublin, 1978. (Mimeographed.)

―――. "Teología y liberación." ISAL 3 (1970): 2–5.

―――. *Toward a Christian Political Ethics.* Philadelphia: Fortress Press, 1983.

―――. "Whatever Happened to Theology?" *Christianity and Crisis* 35 (May 1975): 111–12.

Miller, David. *Social Justice.* Oxford: Clarendon Press, 1976.

Miranda, José Porfirio. *Being and the Messiah: The Message of St. John.* Translated by John Eagleson. New York: Orbis Books, 1977.

―――. *Communism in the Bible.* Translated by Robert R. Barr. Maryknoll, N.Y.: Orbis Books, 1982.

―――. *Hambre y sed de justicia.* 2d ed. México: n.p., 1972.

―――. *Marx and the Bible: A Critique of the Philosophy of Oppression.* Translated by John Eagleson. Maryknoll, N.Y.: Orbis Books, 1974.

―――. *Marx y la Biblia: Crítica a la filosofía de la opresión.* Salamanca: Ediciones Sígueme, 1975.

Nisbet, Charles T. *Latin America: Problems in Economic Development.* New York: The Free Press, 1969.

Nozick, Robert. *Anarchy, State and Utopia.* New York: Basic Books, Inc., 1974.

Ogden, Schubert M. *Faith and Freedom: Toward a Theology of Liberation.* Nashville: Abingdon, 1979.

Okun, Arthur M. *Equality and Efficiency: The Big Tradeoff.* Washington, D.C.: The Brookings Institution, 1975.

Packenham, Robert A. *Liberal America and the Third World.* Princeton, N.J.: Princeton University Press, 1973.

Perelman, Chaim. *The Idea of Justice and the Problems of Argument.* New York: Humanities Press, 1963.

―――. *Justice.* New York: Random House, 1967.

Petit, Philip. *Judging Justice: An Introduction to Contemporary Political Philosophy.* London: Routledge and Kegan Paul, 1980.

Plant, Raymond; Lesser, Harry; and Taylor-Gooby, Peter. *Political Philosophy and Social Welfare: Essays on the Normative Basis of Welfare Provision.* London: Routledge and Kegan Paul, 1980.

Portes, Alejandro. "On the Sociology of National Development." *American Journal of Sociology* 82 (1976): 55–85.

Prebisch, Raúl. "Los obstáculos al mercado común de América Latina." In *Integración de América Latina.* Edited by Miguel S. Wionczek. México: Fondo de Cultura Económica, 1964. Pp. 136–51.

————. *Nueva política comercial para el desarrollo*. México: Fondo de Cultura Económica, 1964.

Quijano, Aníbal. "Dependencia, cambio social y urbanización en Latinoamerica." In *América Latina: Ensayos de interpretación sociológico-política*. Edited by Fernando H. Cardoso and Francisco Weffort. Chile: Editorial Universitaria S.A., 1970. Pp. 96–140.

Rawls, John. *A Theory of Justice*. Cambridge, Mass.: Belknap Press of Harvard University, 1973.

Rescher, Nicholas. *Distributive Justice*. New York: Bobbs-Merrill, 1966.

Ross, Alf. "Directives and the 'Validity' of Law." In *The Nature of Law: Readings in Legal Philosophy*. Edited by M. P. Golding. New York: Random House, 1966. Pp. 134–43.

Rostow, Walt Whitman. *The Stages of Economic Growth, A Non-Communist Manifesto*. Cambridge: Cambridge University Press, 1962.

Segundo, Juan Luis. *De la sociedad a la teología*. Buenos Aires: Ediciones Carlos Lohlé, 1970.

————. "Derechos humanos, evangelización e ideología." In *Carter y la lógica del imperialismo*. Vol. 2. Edited by Hugo Assmann. Costa Rica: EDUCA, 1978. Pp. 339–53.

————. *The Liberation of Theology*. Translated by John Drury. Maryknoll, N.Y.: Orbis Books, 1976.

Sobrino, Jon. *Christology at the Crossroads*. Translated by John Drury. Maryknoll, N.Y.: Orbis Books, 1978.

Sotelo, Ignacio. *Sociología de América Latina: Estructuras y problemas*. Madrid: Editorial Tecnos, 1975.

Stavenhagen, Rudolfo. "Seven Fallacies about Latin America." In *Latin America, Reform or Revolution?* Edited by James Petras and Maurice Zeitlin. Greenwich, Conn.: Fawcett Publications, 1968. Pp. 13–31.

Stein, Stanley J.; and Stein, Barbara H. *La herencia colonial de América Latina*. Translated by Alejandro Licona. México: Siglo Veintiuno Editores S.A., 1973.

Tamez, Elsa; and Trinidad, Saúl, eds. *Capitalismo: Violencia y anti-vida. La opresión de las mayorías y la domesticación de los dioses*. 2 vols. Costa Rica: EDUCA, 1978.

Vasconi, Tomás Amadeo; Dos Santos, Theotonio; Kaplan, Marcos; and Jaguaribe, Helio. *La crisis de desarrollismo y la nueva dependencia*. Compiled by José Matos Mar. Buenos Aires: Amorrortu Editores S.C.A., 1972.

Vlastos, Gregory. "Justice and Equality." In *Social Justice*. Edited by Richard Brandt. Englewood Cliffs, N.J.: Prentice-Hall, 1962. Pp. 31–72.